Great Gardens from Everyday Plants

How to create a beautiful garden with easy-to-find plants from your local nursery or garden center

Anne Halpin

A Fireside Book
Published by Simon & Schuster

New York • London • Toronto • Sydney • Tokyo • Singapore

FIRESIDE
Simon & Schuster Building
Rockefeller Center
1230 Avenue of the Americas
New York, New York 10020

FIRESIDE and colophon are registered trademarks of
Simon & Schuster Inc.

Designed by Peter Loewer

Illustrations by Fran Gallagher

Photographs by Tom Moyer

Manufactured in the United States of America

10   9   8   7   6   5   4   3   2   1

Library of Congress Cataloging in Publication Data

Halpin, Anne Moyer.
    Great gardens from everyday plants : how to create a beautiful
garden with easy-to-find plants from your local nursery or garden
center / Anne Halpin.
        p.   cm.
    Includes bibliographical references and indexes.
    1. Landscape gardening.   2. Plants, Ornamental.   3. Gardens.
4. Gardening.   I. Title.
SB473.H296   1993
635.9—dc20   92-35609
                                                                  CIP

ISBN: 0-671-79697-6

To Mom and Dad,
who first taught me how to garden

Acknowledgments

There are numerous people besides the author whose knowledge and talents go into the creation of a book. I especially want to thank the creative team who worked so hard to get this book finished under a very tight schedule, and who did such an outstanding job: my brother, Tom Moyer, for the photographs; Fran Gallagher, for her imaginative illustrations; and Peter Loewer, for the graphic design and much helpful advice.

I join with Tom in thanking The Flower Mart, Wayside Garden Center, and The Village Gardener, in Nashville, Tennessee, and the residents of Nashville, who grow beautiful flowers and allowed him access to photograph them.

I would also like to thank Kim Solomito and Jon Malkmes, of the Fickle Pickle Florist in Southampton, New York, for answering many questions about plants and the plant trade.

Finally, thanks once again to my husband, John White, for his neverending support and encouragement.

Contents

Introduction

The process of growth is forever mysterious, and gardens can be places of awe and wonder. But there's nothing mysterious about gardening—it is not an arcane art. Anyone can garden, and I believe that everyone should, even if the "garden" is just a couple of plants in flowerpots. Gardening is the most rewarding of activities, giving us a chance to reestablish our connection with the natural world, and affording us the satisfaction of nurturing our own little bit of the Earth.

Gardening can be as simple or as complex as you make it; there is certainly much to be learned in the garden. You could spend a lifetime studying plants and how to grow them and still barely scratch the surface of the subject. But a lifetime of knowledge is not required to be a good gardener.

Gardening can be the passion of a life, and the gardener a relentless seeker of knowledge, on a quest for new and different plants, and better ways to grow them. But gardening can also be simply a pleasant way to spend one's free time, an excuse to get outside and enjoy the sunshine and fresh air, an enjoyable activity that is healthy for the gardener and for the Earth.

The aim of this book (and really, of all the books I write) is to demystify the process of gardening and make it accessible to everyone. This book is not for the passionate seekers. It is instead for everyone with an appreciation of plants and an inclination to try their hand at growing some. It is for new gardeners, and for more experienced growers who don't have the time or the discipline to plan ahead and order seeds and plants by mail. It is for all of us who find ourselves at a local nursery or garden center on the first warm day in spring—along with all our neighbors—trying to figure out which plants to buy and what to do with them when we get them home.

You know the scene: it's a warm Saturday in May (or April, or even March, depending on where you live) and you suddenly realize it's time to plant the garden. Memorial Day is right around the corner and you want your yard to be pretty for the start of the summer season. You hop in your car and drive to the local garden center, where you encounter a scene of near pandemonium. The place is mobbed with people, and you see table after table of little plants in six-packs, flats, and pots. You wander around trying to decide what to buy, being jostled by the crowd. Your eyes glaze over, your nerves begin to fray—all you want is to get out of there. Finally you grab a couple of flats of marigolds and petunias and beat a retreat. Back home, you plunk the plants into the ground and wonder why the garden looks so boring. You probably vow that next year you will order all your plants from catalogs, knowing full well that next year you will go through the same frustrating experience all over again.

But it doesn't have to be this way. From the midst of the garden center's chaos can come order. It *is* possible to create a beautiful garden from ordinary plants, and it is the intent of this book to show you how. Garden designers and horticulturists tend to consider some plants cliches because everybody grows them. While there is much to be said for creativity and individual expression in the garden, I don't believe it is necessary to grow exotic plants in order to achieve satisfaction. Even the most common plants, when artfully arranged and grown with care, can make a perfectly lovely garden. It is the act of gardening that is most important.

Although you will not find many rare and exotic plants at the local garden center, you will find enough choices to allow you to create something pretty with a minimum of time and effort. You may not be in the vanguard of horticultural fashion, but you will be able to keep up with the major trends. By all means allow yourself to have a little fun and try something new in your garden each year. Garden centers stock the plants for which they perceive the greatest market, and the choices are expanding. Most now carry a reasonable selection of perennials and herbs, as well as annuals and vegetables. And now that ornamental grasses have gained popularity, they are appearing in garden centers as well. Shrubs, trees, and vines are sold as well, but woody plants are not covered in this book. As gardeners become more sophisticated in their tastes, the market responds. It is becoming easier, for example, to purchase flowers in individual colors rather than only in flats of mixed colors.

So let us imagine that it is spring, and you are resigned to the inevitable. The question is, with all those choices at the garden center, how do you decide what to buy? The plants are so small that you can't envision what they will look like when fully grown, or how much space they will take up. And how do you put them together in a pleasing way? That's where this book comes in. It's a step-by-step guide to creating a beautiful garden with everyday plants found in any garden center. I have attempted to simplify the process of deciding what to grow, buying plants, getting them into the ground, and maintaining them in peak condition. This book has something of a northeastern bias, because that's where I'm from, but many of the plants and most of the basic techniques are the same no matter where you live, although their timing will vary from one region to another.

However large or small your garden, however much or little time you have to spend, whatever the size of your budget, you will, I hope, find the information in this book helpful. Throughout the text you will find charts and checklists to help make the process easier. There is also an appendix containing lists of plants for a host of different purposes, which you can use for quick reference, and a glossary of helpful terms.

Chapter One gives some pointers on preparing for a visit to the garden center. A little advance planning—however minimal—makes it a lot easier to decide what to buy. Even if you just take fifteen minutes to look at the garden's location and choose a color scheme, you will at least have some basic guidelines to follow in picking out plants. The more you plan ahead, the easier it will be to choose plants. Careful planning will also produce the best-looking garden. This chapter will tell you what to consider before you buy plants, and which decisions to make in advance.

Chapter Two covers basics of garden design: how to combine plants to good effect by considering their size and shape, color, texture, and function in the overall design. The text covers the design of container plantings as well as beds and borders in the ground. In addition to basic design, there is a section on special effects that can be created with particular types of plants. This chapter also explains how to factor into the design such practical considerations as how much time and effort you want to put into the garden, how to match plants to the growing conditions that exist on your property, and how to figure out how many plants to buy. The chapter ends with an illustrated compendium of design ideas to inspire your creative efforts.

Chapter Three is about shopping for plants. You will find advice on how to locate a good garden center, how to choose the healthiest plants at the optimum size and stage of development, and how to make substitutions if some of the plants you want are not available. This chapter also discusses when to buy plants, and how to treat them until you can get them into the ground.

Chapter Four deals with planting and maintenance techniques, including when and how to plant, care of new transplants, planting in containers, watering, fertilizing, weeding, mulching, deadheading and pinching back, controlling pests and diseases, and maintaining healthy soil.

Chapter Five is a concise guide to flowers and herbs found in most garden centers. For each plant you will find the common and botanical names, a brief description including height, color range, texture and leaf shape, and the overall look of the plant, the plant's function in the garden (such as background or edging), and any special qualities the plant may possess. Each plant's cultural needs are outlined as well.

A Few Words About Plant Names

Chapter Five is organized alphabetically, in most cases according to the botanical names of the flowers included (herbs are listed under their common names). For the sake of convenience I have included an Index of Common Plant Names in the back of the book, immediately preceding the general index, to enable

you to easily locate in Chapter Five plants for which you do not know the scientific names.

Botanical nomenclature may seem confusing, and unnecessary for gardeners to learn, but don't be intimidated by it. Learning the botanical names of the plants you want to grow will actually make them less—not more—confusing. Common names vary from place to place and person to person. One gardener's periwinkle is another gardener's myrtle. And the name myrtle is given to at least two very different plants. But if you know you want *Vinca minor* there is little chance you will get the wrong plant. The botanical name is the same, no matter what country you happen to be in, or what part of the country. Botanists do argue among themselves about scientific names, and sometimes plants are reclassified, often to the dismay of gardeners and nursery people (this happened not too long ago with the genus *Chrysanthemum,* some of whose well-known members have been split off into new genera). But botanical names are still the surest way of identifying plants.

Each plant is given two Latin names, one indicating the genus (the generic name) and the other identifying the particular species. Both names are written in italics, with the genus name capitalized. Generic and specific names may describe some quality of the plant or commemorate an eminent person in the field. For example, the name *Pelargonium,* the genus of the common bedding geranium, is derived from an ancient Greek word for stork, and refers to the shape of the seed capsules, which were thought to resemble a stork's beak. The *Fuchsia* was named in honor of Leonhart Fuchs, a sixteenth century German herbalist and doctor.

A plant may also be given a third name to distinguish it from other variants of the same genus and species. If the variety occurs naturally its name is written in italics and preceded by the abbreviation var., in Roman type, for variety. If the variety was developed in cultivation, it is known as a cultivar, a shortened form of cultivated variety, and is indicated in Roman and enclosed in single quotes or preceded by the abbreviation cv. Varieties of a species may differ from one another in color, in the number of petals of their flowers, their growth habit (a weeping form, for instance), their size (such as a dwarf), leaf pattern (as in variegated forms), or other characteristics. In informal usage, the term variety may also be used to refer to plants that are actually cultivars. In this book I have often used the two terms rather loosely in this way.

Plants within a species are similar in structure, share a common heritage, and remain the same from one generation to the next. A genus is a group of closely related species. Related genera are in turn grouped into families.

A multiplication sign before a genus or species name (sometimes erroneously depicted as a letter X), indicates that the plant is a hybrid.

Like most other aspects of gardening, botanical names really are not so difficult if you take a little time to learn to understand them. But whatever names you choose to use for the plants you grow, the most important thing is to grow them.

Composting for a Better Garden

No matter which plants you choose to grow, one of the best things you can do to help them grow strong and vigorous is to add compost to your soil each year. It is one of the most effective soil conditioners there is, and it's impossible to have too much of it. Compost adds organic matter and nutrients to the soil, improving its texture, fertility, drainage, and water retention. And composting allows us to give back some of what we take from the earth, by recycling plant wastes and, if we wish, some of our household garbage as well.

Compost is easy to make, and, contrary to popular opinion, when properly made a compost pile does not produce an unpleasant smell when the material is decomposing. You can make compost from any of a number of organic materials.

Constructing a compost pile according to certain traditional guidelines will allow materials to break down quickly and odorlessly. The finished compost will be dark brown and crumbly, with an earthy smell. Here are some simple directions for making compost.

It is best to make compost in some sort of enclosure. You can purchase compost bins and tumblers at many garden centers and hardware stores. Or you can make your own container. You might opt for a simple cylindrical pen made from chicken wire or hardware cloth. Or you can build a bin from scrap lumber, snow fencing, concrete blocks, or bricks. A wire cylinder can simply be lifted when it is time to turn the pile. If you build a more permanent bin or pen, make a door to allow access to the compost, or simply construct a three-sided structure instead of a completely closed container.

In the bottom of the compost container, lay a few inches of small tree branches or brush, to allow air to circulate underneath the pile. Put down a layer of green plant debris or household garbage 2 to 4 inches deep. You can compost vegetable peelings, coffee grounds, and eggshells, but do *not* use meat products, fats, oils, or pet droppings. Next, put down 2 to 4 inches of dry materials, preferably shredded into small pieces: dry leaves, straw, or dry plant material, for example.

If you wish you can put a 1- to 2-inch layer of livestock manure or soil on top of the dry material. Repeat the layers, dampening each layer as you build—the material should be moist but not soggy. You can use a compost activator if you like; these products contain bacteria to help get the decomposition process started, and several are on the market, readily available in garden centers.

It is okay to compost weeds, as long as they have not yet gone to seed; weeds with seeds will be spread throughout the garden with the compost. Fresh grass clippings are also useful, but spread them in a thin layer in the compost heap; if you pile on a thick layer of green clippings they will turn slimy and smelly. If you want to make compost from nothing but dry leaves, moisten them until they are about as damp as a wrung-out sponge, and alternate 2- to 4-inch layers of leaves with 1 to 2 inches of uncomposted livestock manure, or another nitrogen source such as blood meal.

For the quickest results, turn the pile with a pitchfork at least once a week to mix the materials and keep the compost going. The center of the pile should become quite hot. When turning, fork material from the outer edges of the pile into the center. If the pile seems dry, water it. The compost should be ready to use in a month or two.

You can also make perfectly good compost if you turn the pile less frequently, or not at all. The decomposition process will just take longer. Compost is ready to use when the individual ingredients are no longer recognizable, but have broken down into a dark-colored mass that is easily crumbled.

Add a $\frac{1}{2}$- to 1-inch layer of compost to your garden every year, as recommended in Chapter Four, to keep the soil in good condition and to provide the optimum growing medium for your plants.

Creating and tending a beautiful garden of healthy, vigorous plants is among the most rewarding of leisure activities. Even if your garden consists only of a few plants in pots or windowboxes, watching those plants grow is good for the soul. I hope the information in this book will encourage you to garden and increase your pleasure in doing so.

Chapter One

Before You Buy the Plants

To make the most of a trip to the garden center, make some decisions about the garden before you go.

Ideally, you should draw a map—or at least a rough sketch—of the garden, and list the kinds of plants you will put in different spots. If you are starting a new garden you need to decide where to locate it, and make a drawing of the site. Measure the area with a tape measure and calculate the approximate square footage of the garden-to-be, so you can figure out how many plants you will need. A drawing done to scale will be most accurate (you might use, for example, one-quarter to one-half inch on the drawing to represent one foot of garden space), but a sketch reflecting the approximate dimensions of the garden will do.

It is important to decide in advance where the garden will go so that you can choose plants that will grow in the conditions present in the garden location, and that will best serve the purposes for which you need them. Planning ahead will save you time and money, as well as untold amounts of the frustration that arises from planting unsuitable plants in a poorly chosen garden location.

Places for Gardens

You may think of a garden as a rectangular plot of ground in the backyard, where vegetables are raised, or as a bed of annuals and foundation shrubs at the front of the house. But there are all sorts of places you can put a garden or even a few plants.

One approach is to plant in island beds carved out of an expanse of lawn. Instead of the usual rectangle that is so common for vegetable gardens, resembling a miniature farm field with its straight, widely spaced rows of plants, you can make island beds that are circular, elliptical, square, triangular, kidney-shaped, or freeform. You can put beds in a front, back, or side yard, in front of a hedge, fence, or wall. Instead of planting in rows, you can plant in gently flowing drifts, concentric rings (in a round garden), blocks, or strict geometric patterns. The way you set out plants can create a naturalistic, wild-landscape look,

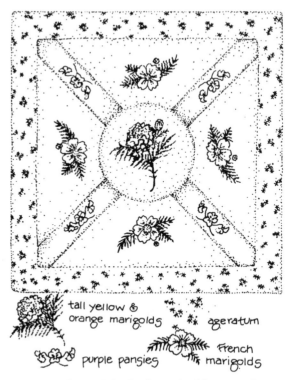

tall yellow & orange marigolds   ageratum

purple pansies   French marigolds

A small formal bed of marigolds, pansies, and ageratum in a geometric pattern.

a tapestry effect reminiscent of Victorian carpet bedding schemes, the romantic jumble of a cottage garden, or a neat, controlled, formal appearance.

Instead of taking the form of a bed, a garden can be stretched into a border, narrower than it is long, to divide different areas of your yard, or to separate your property from your neighbor's.

You can plant in the more or less public parts of your property, like that strip of grass between the sidewalk and the street, or the entrance to a driveway.

At the end of the driveway, a small patch holds pink petunias and purple balloonflowers; blue morning glories climb the lamppost.

Think about planting along the driveway, or the pavement that leads to your door, to welcome visitors. Or put in a small dooryard garden of flowers by the front door, or a patch of flowers, herbs, and vegetables by the back door.

You can hide an unsightly wall by planting small plants in pockets of dirt between its stones or concrete blocks, or by growing trailing plants in containers set on top of the wall, or in the ground immediately behind the top of a retaining wall.

Plant groundcovers amid and between paving stones in a path. Train vines to cover a trellis or arbor. Soften the base of a tree by surrounding it with flowers.

Think about growing some plants in containers, too, even if you already have a garden in the ground. Containers full of colorful flowers and aromatic herbs bring the pleasures of plants right up close where you can enjoy them. Large tubs of plants offer a gracious welcome to visitors when placed beside a gate, or on the steps leading up to the front porch. Group pots and large tubs of plants on a porch, city rooftop, deck, or patio to provide a leafy retreat for outdoor dining, reading, or other pursuits. Setting smaller pots of blooming plants and foliage on the steps between the deck and the yard can help create an inviting entry to your outdoor garden "room." Windowboxes bring a special charm all their own, softening the severe facade of an apartment building, or dressing up a porch. Mount the boxes on or immediately below windowsills, or on a porch railing. If you are using windowboxes on a porch, you can suspend hanging baskets of trailing vines above them to create a living privacy screen, and provide welcome shade on a hot summer day. See the end of Chapter Two for an assortment of more specific design ideas.

Windowboxes are easy to plant and maintain, and as appealing on a city apartment building as on a country cottage.

It is difficult for many of us to visualize what a garden might look like in any given location, but here is a risk-free way to experiment with garden placement. Start by taking some black and white photographs of your house from different angles. Stand on the sidewalk in front of the house to get a street-side perspective. This is how passersby and visitors will see your garden, if it is out front. Take some photos looking out through your windows, too, or standing right outside the windows—this is how you and your family will most often see your garden. When you have the photos developed, pick the best views and have several

enlargements made of each. Then use a felt-tipped marker to draw in the garden on the photo where you think you might like to put it. You can experiment with different locations and different shapes. To save on the expense of getting lots of enlargements, you could get just one or two prints made, then make paper cutouts of potential gardens, and lay them on top of the photo. Or you could perhaps even cut pictures of gardens you like from magazines and try placing them on the photo of your yard.

The Best Site for a Garden

Remember that the farther from the house the garden is located, the more work it will be to maintain. You will have to carry to the garden necessary tools, and supplies for fertilizing or spraying for bugs. You will also need longer hoses to reach a water source. It will be easier to forget to weed, water, and deadhead (remove faded flowers) if you don't pass by the garden as you come and go from the house. Putting the garden out of sight may also put it out of mind, and it can become overgrown before you know it. A location close to the house will afford maximum enjoyment of the garden, because you will see it often, and will simplify maintenance. But the most important criteria for a garden spot are the environmental conditions it offers. Assess growing conditions on your property carefully when picking out a site for a new garden. A location in full sun (which is defined below) will allow you the greatest choice of plants, although there are plenty of plants that will grow in shade, too.

When you have chosen the location for your garden, the next step is to choose a shape for the garden and think about what kinds of plants you would like to grow. The design process is discussed in more detail in Chapter

Two, but the basis of site selection and plant choices is an understanding of the garden environment. The real secret to successful gardening is to match plants to the conditions available. Study the conditions present in all the parts of your property that you have identified as potential garden sites, so that you will be better able to choose plants that will thrive in your garden.

How much light will be available for plants? Does the location receive full sun, partial shade, or shade? Full sun can be defined as six or more hours of unobstructed sunlight a day. Partial shade is a location that receives two to six hours of direct sun, or lightly dappled sunlight all day. A location receiving less than two hours of sunlight, or only bits of sunshine filtered through a heavier canopy of leaves, or shadowed by a building for part of the day, is considered to be in full shade. If your prospective garden spot is in dense shade, where no sunlight at all reaches the ground, count on growing woodland plants.

In assessing sun availability, remember that the location of the sun in the sky changes over the course of the year. The shifting position of the sun, as well as the presence and absence of leaves on nearby deciduous trees, will create patterns of sun and shade that change as the sun moves across the sky, and days grow

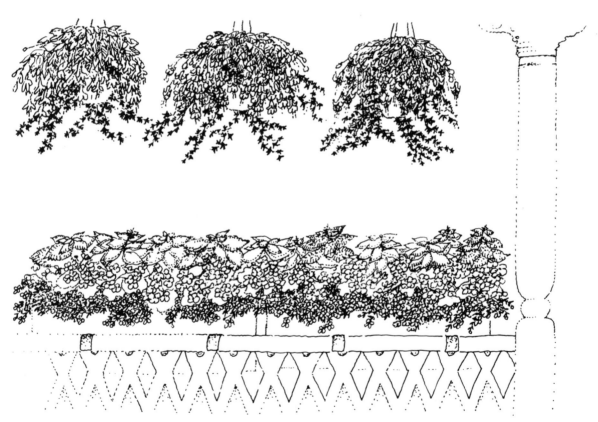

A shady porch becomes a bower when plants are added. Here, hanging baskets of fuchsias and ivy are suspended above windowboxes filled with coleus, wax begonias, and lobelia.

longer and shorter. A place that is totally sunny in winter, when the trees are leafless, may be partly or fully shaded in summer. In winter the sun reaches its southernmost point in the sky for those of us who live in the Northern Hemisphere. As spring progresses the sun travels ever northward, riding higher in the sky and reaching its most northerly point at the summer solstice, the longest day of the year, around the twenty-first of June. After that date the sun begins to slip southward again, and by the end of summer you can see a decided difference in the quality of its light. By late summer and on into autumn, the sun is lower in the sky and less intense than it was in June, and the days have grown noticeably shorter. Being aware of the changing light patterns across your property will help you in choosing a garden location and in selecting plants that will grow in it.

Soil

Soil is another important consideration in planning a garden and choosing plants. What is the soil like in your garden-to-be? Is it dense and clayey? Light and sandy? Crumbly and loamy? Is it fertile or low in nutrients? Acid or alkaline? A dark brown, crumbly soil that contains plenty of organic matter and nutrients, with a pH acceptable to the majority of plants, is the optimum growing medium.

Few of us are fortunate enough to start out with soil like this, but any soil can be improved. The first step is to understand what kind of soil you have to work with, and build from there.

Clay soil is usually dark in color—often a reddish brown—tends to form clumps, and feels somewhat sticky or slippery when wet. Clay soils are dense and heavy in texture because the individual particles of clay are very tiny and pack tightly together. Such soils drain slowly because there is little air space between the particles. Clay soils warm and dry out slowly in spring, and are not ready for planting as early as lighter soils. On the positive side, clay soils usually contain more nutrients for plants than do lighter soils, and do not dry out as quickly during spells of dry weather.

Sandy soils have opposite qualities. They are light-colored and loose-textured, sand particles being substantially larger than clay particles. Sandy soils are generally very well-drained and easy to work, and seldom suffer from compaction. They dry out very quickly during a drought, and may be lacking in nutrients because the rapid drainage leaches them from the soil.

Loamy soils—the ideal type for gardeners—are a mixture of sand and clay particles, along with silt. They are crumbly-textured, drain well while still retaining enough moisture for plants, and are naturally fertile. If you are lucky enough to have loamy soil, consider yourself blessed.

It is important to know what sort of soil you have to work with in order to properly manage it and to choose the best plants to grow in it. It is wise to get a soil test before planting a new garden. You can get soil tested through your local USDA County Extension office (they will also give you directions on taking the necessary soil samples). Or you can work with a private laboratory testing service, or purchase a do-it-yourself soil test kit. A soil test will inform you about the soil's structural composition, content of organic matter, the amount of the three major nutrients—nitrogen, phosphorus, and potassium—trace element content, and pH. The USDA and some other testing services will make recommendations on what to do to improve the quality of the soil.

No matter what kind of soil you have, it can be improved by the addition of organic matter. Adding organic matter to clay soils lightens the dense texture (organic matter particles are larger than clay particles), improving drainage and aeration. In sandy soils, organic matter adds body, improves the ability of the soil to hold water, and contributes some nutrients as well. Whether or not you are a strictly organic gardener, you should add organic matter to your soil each year, as described in Chapter Four. If your soil is already of high quality, regular additions of organic matter will help to keep it that way.

pH is a measure of the soil's acidity or alkalinity. It is measured on a fourteen-point scale, with 7.0 representing neutral, a soil that is neither acid nor alkaline. Most plants grow best in soil that is mildly acidic to nearly neutral, although most can tolerate a range of pH. Some plants, however, have particular needs for acid or alkaline soils, without which they will not thrive. Azaleas and rhododendrons are among the most familiar acid-lovers, while baby's breath is a plant that prefers alkaline soil. Throughout this book, and especially in Chapter Five, pH is mentioned only where plants need a pH within a specific range. In most cases, a mildly acidic to neutral pH is acceptable.

It is best to choose plants that thrive in the natural pH of your soil, rather than trying to adjust soil pH to suit plants. You can alter the pH of soil to a modest degree by incorporating acidic materials into alkaline soil or alkaline materials into acid soil. Large amounts of ground limestone or wood ashes, for example, can raise the pH of acid soil, while cottonseed meal or acid peat moss can slightly lower the pH of alkaline soil. But attempting to make major changes in your soil's pH will probably prove to be a losing battle. It is easier and better in the long run to work with the soil's natural tendency to be acid, neutral, or alkaline.

Other Factors to Consider

Another consideration in choosing a garden site is the drainage, which is determined by the lay of the land as well as the soil type. Think about whether the potential site tends in general to be wet or dry. A garden at the bottom of a hill will collect water (and cold air in winter), while a higher location will drain quickly. If there are low spots on your property where water collects and stands after heavy rain, try to avoid putting the garden there. If such a poorly drained spot is the only available location for a garden, you will have to install drainage tiles or a layer of gravel beneath the soil to improve the drainage, or grow plants that prefer moist conditions, such as iris and astilbe or, in extreme cases, bog plants from a water garden nursery.

If the drainage problem is not so severe, constructing raised beds in which to garden can provide the well-drained environment most plants need. You can simply mound up new soil to a depth of a foot or so on top of what's already there. A blend of good topsoil, compost, and peat moss or sharp builder's sand will provide a humusy, porous, moisture-retentive but well-drained growing medium for plants. Keep the soil in the raised beds in place by sloping the sides or by edging the beds with stone, bricks, or lumber treated with a preservative that is nontoxic to plants. Copper and zinc naphthenate are two preservatives that are generally considered safe to use around plants.

There are some additional environmental factors that may influence the growing environment in and immediately around the garden—its microclimate, in other words.

If your property is exposed to frequent strong winds, look for a position that is afforded some protection by a windbreak—a barrier between the garden and the direction from which the prevailing winds blow. A windbreak can take the form of plants; a row of evergreen shrubs, perhaps, or a mixed hedgerow planting of small trees and shrubs of graduated heights, or a tall privet hedge. Or the windbreak can be a wall or fence of open construction, such as a picket fence, that allows air to pass through it. A solid wall is likely to create strange air flow patterns that may damage your plants nearly as much as the unobstructed wind. If no windbreak currently exists, you can plant or install one. Consult a good book on landscape design for more information on siting and installing windbreaks.

In a harsh climate, putting a garden bed next to the south-facing wall of the house can be a good idea. The house will shelter the garden from the north, and may create a microclimate where growing conditions are milder than in the surrounding area. Such a garden may have conditions equivalent to those in gardens located a full hardiness zone farther south than the zone in which the garden is actually located. You may be able to grow some perennials that most of your neighbors cannot, which some gardeners find immensely satisfying.

If the house is constructed of brick or stone, or the garden is located immediately next to another masonry surface, such as a stone wall, temperatures are moderated in winter. Brick and stone provide what is known as thermal mass. They absorb and store heat during sunny days, and release the stored warmth back into the air slowly at night, providing a buffer against sharp, rapid temperature swings that can be difficult for overwintering plants. The same principle operates in summer as well, however, and the location may become too hot for sensitive plants on summer afternoons.

The presence of a large body of water nearby also modifies the climate. Gardens near the ocean or a large lake will warm more slowly in spring and cool more slowly in fall than gardens farther inland. On coastal Long Island, my garden is in USDA Zone 7, but when I lived in Pennsylvania my garden was in Zone 6, even though it was farther south. One problem coastal gardeners must contend with, however, is salt, which is carried in the wind, even to gardens not right by the beach. Gardeners close to the sea can establish shelter belts of salt-tolerant trees and shrubs to protect their gardens, but all gardeners in seashore communities need to learn which plants can and cannot tolerate the salt and winds that are a part of the coastal environment.

Finally, if your garden spot is in a shady location, look for local factors that may affect the degree and quality of the shade. A high canopy of small leaves on tall trees will provide an open, dappled shade that is hospitable to more plants than a dense canopy which allows little sunlight to reach the ground. White or light-colored surfaces nearby can reflect additional light into the garden area.

When you have assessed the environmental conditions in your yard, the best spot for your garden will be wherever the best combination of conditions exists. Choose a place that receives the maximum available sunlight during the growing season, where the soil is in the best condition, and where adequate moisture is present, or you will be able to water easily. But never forget that you can have a successful garden almost anywhere if you improve the growing conditions and choose plants that will grow in the conditions you have to offer.

If several places meet the environmental criteria, you can go on to factor in some aesthetic considerations as you decide where to put the garden. How would a garden in a particular spot relate to other architectural features on the property, such as the house, garage, fences, walls, sidewalks, and driveways? From what vantage point will the garden most often be viewed—from the street, from inside the house, from somewhere in the yard? Will you want to use the garden as outdoor living space in good weather? If you plan to use it for outdoor entertaining, make it convenient to the kitchen. If you want the garden to be a kind of sanctuary, a quiet retreat, a less-traveled location farther from the house would serve better.

Garden Location Planner

Here is a summary of factors to consider when choosing a location for a new garden. All are explained in some detail in the text.

○ Is the site in full sun, partial shade, or shade? Does the amount of light change drastically between spring and fall, or in winter (important in the case of shrubs)?

○ What type of soil is present—sandy, clay, or loam?

○ Is the soil pH acid, alkaline, or neutral?

○ How fertile is the soil?

○ Does the soil tend toward wetness or dryness?

○ Is the site at the top or bottom of a hill?

○ Are there any local factors present that will influence the microclimate in the immediate vicinity of the garden?

  • hedges or hedgerows that serve as a windbreak

  • solid walls or fences that could create unusual wind patterns

  • the south-facing wall of a house that could provide shelter

  • white and light-colored surfaces that reflect light

  • masonry surfaces that radiate heat at night

  • a large nearby body of water that will moderate the climate (if that water is the ocean, beware of salt carried in the air, and create a shelter belt to protect the garden)

○ What is your climate like? How long is the frost-free growing season? Approximately when do you get your last frost in spring, and your first frost in fall?

What Kind of Garden for You?

When you know where to put the garden, you can start thinking about what kind of garden you want to have. Before you start to design a garden bed or border, it helps to think through what you want from the garden. Here are some things to consider:

Why do you want a garden? Simply to add color to the landscape? To have flowers to cut or dry? Herbs to use in cooking? Do you want plantings to create privacy? To make a sheltered place for reading, picnicking, or other outdoor activities?

What sort of style will work best for you? A city townhouse may be best served by a formal garden of neatly maintained plants in a controlled, elegant setting. A country house looks better with a more informal design—a cottage garden, perhaps, or a naturalistic planting. A contemporary home would be nicely complemented by a bold garden of sculptural plants.

Do you want to have flowers primarily in summer, or do you want the garden to be interesting in spring, fall, and winter as well? Planning for seasonal interest is discussed in Chapter Two.

What colors do you want in the garden? What colors do you like? What color is your house? Your indoor decorating scheme? Choose colors that harmonize or contrast pleasingly with the indoor colors if you are planning a cutting garden.

How much time and energy will you realistically want or be able to devote to gardening? Be honest with yourself. If you are not going to have much time, grow low-maintenance plants and keep the garden simple. You will find a list of low-maintenance plants in the Appendix.

What is your family or household like? Do you have small children or pets who could wreak havoc with delicate plants, or who could be inadvertently harmed if they are tempted to munch on plants that are poisonous, such as foxglove? If you have kids, would you like to help them plant a special little garden of their own, with plants that are colorful, fast, and easy to grow?

If all this sounds confusing, read Chapter Two. And look over the plant descriptions in Chapter Five to see which ones sound appealing. Then go to the garden center or nursery and look at them. Color photographs in books, magazines, and seed and nursery catalogs are helpful, but there is no substitute for seeing the real thing. If you plan to buy young plants in cell packs or flats, look around the garden center to see if there are older specimens in bigger pots, to get a better idea of what the plants will look like as they grow.

Make a list of the plants you would like to grow, and approximately how many of each you will need, before you go on a buying trip. Chapter Three contains information on estimating how many plants you will need to fill a given space.

Prepare the garden before you buy the plants. See Chapter Four for details. It is time-consuming to care for a whole bunch of little plants in individual cell packs. They need water often, especially when the weather is quite warm. It is best not to buy them until you are ready to plant them.

Circumventing the Planning Process

If you just haven't got the time or discipline to plan the garden properly, you can fall back on what might be described as the buy-plant-buy more-plant again method. Go to the garden center and buy just a couple of packs or flats of one or two kinds of plants (start with tall plants for the back of the garden). Plant them, then see how much space you have left, and figure out what other plants might look good with them. Then buy some more plants. This is a piecemeal approach, but at least you will be able to gradually assemble a reasonable-looking garden. If you will be growing perennials and do not feel particularly pressed for time, you could assemble your garden over a period of several years, putting in a few plants each year to build the garden a bit at a time. It really is far better to take the time to plan, but if you are just not up to the task, try either of these approaches.

When you are picking out the plants, look at the little plastic label stuck into the container for the plant's sun/shade preference, its mature height, and its flower color. If the plants at your local garden center don't have these labels or tags, take this book with you when you shop, or go to a different garden center. Bear in mind, though, that plant labels are not always entirely accurate. The label may specify as perennial a plant that must be grown as an annual in your climate, although the same plant may well be perennial in warmer zones. In addition, the mature plant may not look exactly like its description on the plant label. Descriptive information can be subjective, especially in regard to color. A flower described as rose-pink, or even just plain pink, on a label may look more like magenta or red-violet to your eye when the plant finally blooms. If you find yourself with some surprises in your garden, try to enjoy them, and chalk them up to experience.

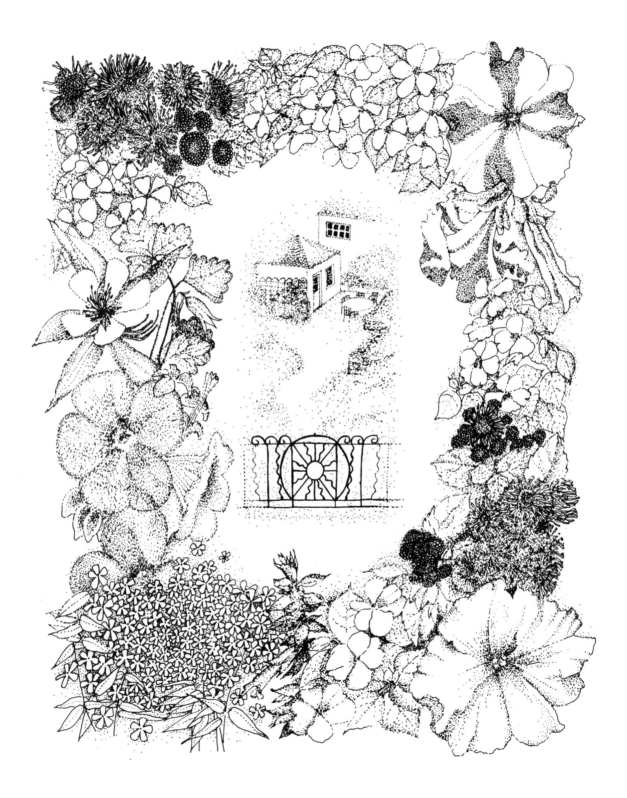

Chapter Two

Designing the Garden

Thoughtful design is what unites a collection of plants into a garden. But garden design, especially in its large, public applications, can be a complex art form, and it can take a lifetime of study and practice to become skilled in its nuances. Luckily for you, you are not designing a garden for a demanding client or a public park. The only audience your garden really has to please is you. So don't be intimidated by the idea of designing a garden from scratch. Use the suggestions in this chapter as a guide to help you solve the problem of what to plant and how to arrange the contents of the garden, but don't look at them as hard and fast rules.

This is your garden, and creating it can be a great deal of fun. Don't be afraid to break the rules, to fly in the face of conventional wisdom if the conventional wisdom does not appeal to you. And don't be afraid to make mistakes. Annuals that don't work will be gone at the end of the season, and incongruous or unbecoming perennials can be dug up and moved to a more felicitous location next year.

One of the great joys of gardens is that they are not static, but dynamic; the process of growth and change is continuous. Even a garden made entirely of perennials, or for that matter, trees and shrubs, will look a little bit different every year. If you like to change the look of your garden significantly every year, plant annuals. You will be able to grow totally different plants in different colors each season. If you want variety without widescale replanting, a combination of annuals and perennials will provide some continuity from year to year. Mixing annuals with perennials is an ideal way to have both color all summer long and a certain degree of consistency from one year to the next; it can give you the best of both worlds.

To get design ideas, take the time to look at other gardens. Look closely at your neighbors' gardens; you may be surprised at what you learn. Go to public gardens to see beds and borders of different shapes, styles, and planting schemes. No matter if the local botanic garden is planted on a grand scale while you've got only a postage stamp-sized plot. Zoom in for a close-up view of those expansive beds and borders to seek out pretty combinations of two or three or more plants that you like, to copy at home or to inspire your own plant choices. You can scale down the design by planting fewer of each type of plant than you see in large public gardens. Books and magazines can also be a source of ideas. Page through gardening publications and look at the pictures; color photographs and illustrations can be immensely useful. Lifestyle and travel magazines also often contain photos of exceptional gardens.

When you see plants, combinations of plants, garden layouts and placements you like, make notes so you will remember them. When the time comes to sit down and design your garden, you will probably find yourself with a wealth of ideas to upon which to draw. The Compendium of Design Ideas at the back of this chapter may also prove helpful.

One other piece of advice for new gardeners is to start small. Nothing will discourage you more quickly than a too-large garden that takes more labor and time to maintain than you have to give. By midsummer the weeds will outnumber the flowers and the garden will be a depressing sight. If this is your first garden, plant a small bed with a limited number of plants. You can always expand next year. If you are not ready to make the commitment to digging up a patch of the yard, grow some flowers and herbs in pots, tubs, hanging baskets or windowboxes this year to give yourself a taste of plant parenthood.

Shapes for Beds and Borders

Gardens come in many shapes and sizes, but they all boil down to two basic types: beds and borders. Quite simply, a border is a garden that is longer than it is wide, and that serves as a divider in the landscape, placed to separate an area of lawn from another element. A border might separate the lawn from a driveway, wall, fence, or hedge, one part of the yard from another, or your property from your neighbor's. You can plant a border of shrubs, or flowers, or herbs, or even vegetables. The expansive spaces of large private estates and public gardens often boast sweeping borders hundreds of feet long. Borders on such a vast scale hold thousands of plants and require a full-time staff of gardeners to maintain them. But borders do not have to be this grand. On a small property a border might only be fifty, or even twenty, feet long. A border may be straight or curved, although flowing curves

One good place for a flower border is between a lawn and a driveway.

give a more natural look than a border with rigidly straight edges.

A garden bed is just about any area devoted solely to plants that does not qualify as a border. Beds can be freestanding and surrounded by lawn (these are known as island beds), or they may butt up against a sidewalk, fence, garage, house, or other structure. They can be flat or raised above the level of the surrounding ground, or constructed in a series of terraces. Garden beds can be square, rectangular, circular, elliptical, triangular, kidney-shaped, crescent-shaped, freeform, or in any shape you like. Unusual geometric patterns can be interesting to work with, but bear in mind that such gardens must be carefully planted and scrupulously maintained so that their edges remain well-defined, or else their precise, amusing shapes will not be evident to viewers.

When choosing a shape for a garden bed, consider the architectural style of your house, and its setting. Neat squares and rectangles help to convey a formal, controlled feeling, while sweeping curves and irregular shapes reflect informality. Also consider the garden's location—you might wish to shape the bed to echo a contour or pattern already present in the landscape.

If you will be creating more than one bed, it is usually best to make them all similar to one another, to bring a sense of continuity

A garden doesn't have to be rectangular. Garden beds can be any shape you like: round, square, elliptical, triangular, crescent-shaped, kidney-shaped, semicircular, or even freeform.

Shaping Gardens to Specific Locations

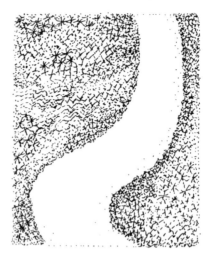

- rectangular beds around pool or patio with tub garden in each corner •

- curved borders along a curved path or driveway •

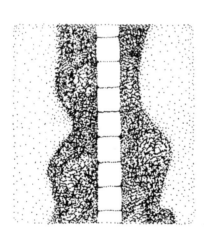

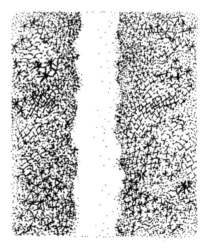

- borders separating a straight paved path from a lawn: one way is to use a straight edge along the path and a curved edge along the lawn •

- to break up the severe line of a straight path, curve the edge of the border and let some plants spill onto the path •

A mixed border of annuals and perennials softens the look of a concrete walkway. This low-maintenance garden includes bright rose portulaca, spiky blue salvia, and the fuzzy silver foliage of lamb's ears.

A border can be as simple as a row of plants along a fence. Shown here are yellow French marigolds, purple coneflower in both its usual dusty rose as well as a white-flowered form, and zinnias in red and orange. In the background stands garden phlox, with its clusters of rose-pink blossoms.

A garden border of tall flowers can separate your property from the street, and offer a pleasant diversion for people walking by. The tall white nicotiana and purple-pink lythrum in this garden effectively screen the view of the street.

*D*rifts of red, white, and pink impatiens shimmer in front of a hot combination of yellow marigolds and scarlet salvia. This all-annuals border is easy and inexpensive to create, and will bloom all summer.

*T*his simple but charming border mixes pink and white petunias behind an edging of lavender sweet alyssum.

A classic and still effective way to use impatiens: massed in front of evergreen shrubs to separate the driveway from the house.

A cool blend of annuals and perennials, this blue and white garden shows how effective a simple color scheme can be. Salvia provides the blue; white flowers include annual spider flower and nicotiana, and perennial achillea. Silver-leaved artemisia and the fluffy plumes of foxtail grass add their soft textures to the composition.

A classic red, white, and blue theme is created in a raised bed garden with red and blue salvia, white garden phlox, and an edging of white-flowered sweet alyssum. Rosy pink bee-balm adds some variation to the mix.

*T*he pot of red impatiens is a great accent for this garden of green and white. As complementary colors, red and green intensify one another when placed in close proximity—reds look redder and greens look greener.

*T*he soil in this circular island bed is mounded toward the center, allowing all the flowers to be easily seen.

*I*n this lovely raised bed garden, pinks and blues are freshened with white and brightened by a dash of red surrounding the central statue. The repetition of flowers through the beds gives a pleasing unity to the garden.

This gardener created a "meadow" of zinnias by scattering the plants far and wide in a sunny garden.

Masses of
Iceland poppies
in mixed colors
create a meadow-
like effect.

*F*ormal carpet beds like these require scrupulous maintenance to retain their perfectly controlled shapes. These spring beds of narcissus and pansies will be replanted with summer bedding plants when the flowers fade and the weather turns warm.

*T*his simple, contemporary formal garden is composed of rectangular island beds of blue salvia, scarlet salvia, and white "vinca" (actually catharanthus) edged with low evergreen hedges.

*H*erbs grow in curved beds on a terrace created by a low stone wall. Note how the morning glories soften the lines of the wooden fence at the back of the garden.

*T*his curved border breaks up the boring straight lines that would be created by a plain lawn butting up against the solid fence.

A border designed in a flowing curved shape looks more natural and less formal than a garden in the form of a square, rectangle, or other geometric shape.

Summer annuals have been removed from this small bed and replaced by an autumn display of mums, pumpkins, and cornstalks.

In a quiet corner, pink and red begonias in the ground and in pots cluster beneath a young redbud tree in the midst of a small garden of perennials and shrubs.

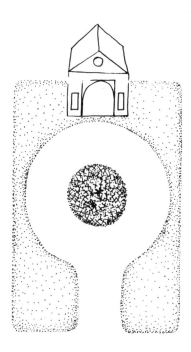

• circular bed in the center of a circular drive •

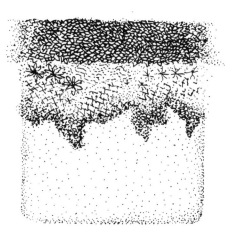

• rectangular border in front of a fence, wall or hedge • let some low plants spill over front edge of border to soften the strict line •

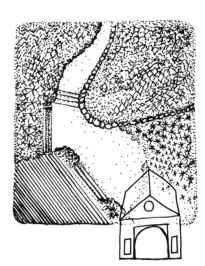

• terraced or unusually shaped beds can break up a small, narrow backyard, and make it seem larger • garden in back is higher than garden closest to house •

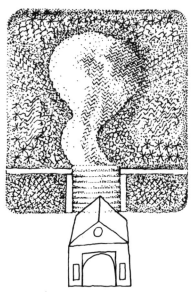

• raised beds close to house •

Designing the Garden / 33

to the landscape. A motley assortment of squares, circles, diamonds, and triangles dotted about the lawn just won't hold together visually.

Different shapes work best in different locations. For example, you might surround a swimming pool with long, rectangular beds, perhaps placing a large potted plant in each corner. For borders next to a curved path, you can curve the side of the borders facing the path to echo the curve of the path. If the path is wide enough, bring the borders right up next to it, and allow some of the low edging plants to spill into the path. If, on the other hand, the path is straight, you might want to give the borders straight edges next to the path, and curve the outer edges where the border meets the lawn. Or curve the borders to break up the severe line of the path for a less formal look. A circular bed works well in the center of a circular driveway. A rectangular bed or border looks quite elegant in front of a wall or fence, but let some of the low-growing plants spill over the front edge of the garden, or curve the front edge instead of leaving it parallel to the line of the wall. If you have a small, narrow property, as so many urban dwellers do, you can break up the space with terraced or unusually angled beds; they will also make the space look bigger. If you plan to create raised beds, it is best to make them square or rectangular; curved shapes are harder to construct, and more expensive.

Containers

Plants in pots can be used in addition to a garden in the ground, or they can form a garden by themselves. Growing some plants in pots can expand your range as a gardener—in summer, you can grow plants that aren't normally

Group containers of plants in different sizes for a garden-like effect on a porch or patio.

hardy outdoors in your area, to add a touch of the tropics to your garden, and bring them indoors when the weather turns cold. You can also grow plants that need special care, or a soil type different from what's available in your garden.

You can use pots to show off special plants—somehow a plant seems more important when it is growing in its own container, especially a decorative, carefully chosen pot. Placing a few potted plants in or near the garden can provide extra color accents. To create the effect of a lush garden in a small space, group lots of potted plants together. Mass the pots on shelved or tiered stands to place the plants at different levels so they will all be visible, or place larger containers holding bigger plants behind smaller pots of shorter plants.

Growing plants in pots allows you to change the colors in your garden from season to season by rotating blooming plants into and out of the display area. And you can easily move plants from one place to another to find an arrangement you really like—you can rearrange the whole garden quite readily, if you wish.

Potted plants grouped on steps or the porch near the front door provide a homey, welcoming feeling, to you and your family and to friends and relatives who come to visit. Windowboxes can make the setting even more delightful, and work their magic in both city and country environments. On a deck, patio,

Pots of pansies and sweet alyssum on the front steps and ivy by the front door welcome visitors.

A decorative container like this handmade clay pot makes even an ordinary geranium special.

or city rooftop, containers full of flowers and greenery can help create a peaceful setting for outdoor dining, reading, or just relaxing after a busy day.

On a porch you can suspend hanging baskets of trailing plants to shade a sitting area and add some charm and color. Placing a row of tall potted plants directly below the hanging baskets will give you a lush, screened effect that can be quite appealing.

Out in the yard, or on a deck, patio, or rooftop, a group of tall plants in large containers can screen off unsightly areas, divide space, create privacy, or provide some shade. Large flowering plants, shrubs, or trellised vines can serve the purpose admirably.

A row of daylilies or other large plants in tubs can divide space or create a screen.

Apartment dwellers can put potted plants on a balcony or fire escape to soften the cityscape. Gardeners with more space can put containers on the paving next to a swimming pool, or along a short driveway or path.

The proportion of plant to container is important. You must of course provide a pot large enough to allow the plant to develop adequate roots to support its growth, but there are aesthetic considerations as well. A large plant in a small pot will look topheavy and uncomfortable, while a small plant in a large pot will get lost. But you can group several smaller plants in a large tub or other container to good effect; just position a taller plant (or two or three) in the center, and surround it with lower growers. You can also group several small plants in individual pots in a larger container to get more visual impact from them. Set small pots in a wicker fernery, windowbox, or tub to create a massed effect. Cover the tops of the pots with sphagnum

moss to hide them. Soak the moss in water before you use it.

See the Appendix for lists of suggested plants for pots, windowboxes, and hanging baskets.

Types of Containers

There are many kinds of containers from which to choose for your plants. The classic is, of course, the unglazed clay flowerpot, which comes in a host of different sizes. You can also find more decorative terra cotta containers—tubs, boxes, vases, strawberry jars, and bowls, for example—in an array of shapes and sizes. A clay pot is still my favorite type of container, both for outdoor and indoor gardens. One drawback to clay, however, is that very large pots are extremely heavy when filled with moist potting medium. If you need to move them you will need assistance. If you choose terra cotta for outdoor use, you will need to keep a close watch on your plants' water needs in summer, because the containers' porous walls allow soil moisture to evaporate readily in hot, dry weather. Also, clay pots must be brought indoors at the end of the growing season where winters are cold, or they are likely to crack before spring.

Many gardeners prefer to pot outdoor plants in plastic containers, which are lightweight, available in many sizes and shapes, and do not allow moisture to evaporate through their walls. Plastic is the material of choice for many hanging baskets because of the weight advantage, and plastic pots are easier to handle in large sizes.

To enjoy the convenience of a simple clay or plastic pot and a decorative look as well, slip the pots into fancy urns, cachepots, or boxes of glazed ceramic, stone, or other material. Bear in mind that if the decorative container has no drainage hole in the bottom, you will need to check after watering the plants to see if excess water has collected in the bottom of the pot and must be removed. For details, see Watering Plants in Containers, in Chapter Four.

Wood is another widely used material, especially for windowboxes and large square or rectangular planter boxes. Wood barrels, half barrels, and tubs have a rustic appeal, and their dark, neutral gray-brown color complements flowers of any hue.

Large urns and vases that seldom need to be moved can be had in stone, faux stone, or concrete, or you can purchase reproductions of Victorian cast iron pieces.

Whatever kind of container you choose, if you will be planting directly in it, rather than using it as a decorative holder for another pot or pots, make sure the container has drainage holes in the bottom. If necessary, punch or drill them yourself. If excess water has no way

to drain from a pot, plant roots will become waterlogged and eventually rot, and the plant will die. If you absolutely must plant in a container without drainage holes, put a couple of inches of fine gravel in the bottom of the pot before adding the potting mix, to provide for some drainage.

Use whatever sort of container strikes your fancy. Just remember if you are using a colored or patterned container to choose plants whose colors will work with the container color. Remember, too, that the fancier the container, the more attention it will call to itself. If you want the plants to be the stars of the show, choose simple pots or tubs rather than oriental jardinieres or planters shaped like cherubs or bunnies.

Color Schemes

Picking out the different colors for a garden is for many of us the most enjoyable part of the planning process. If you give some thought to the color scheme before you make the trip to the garden center it will be that much easier to select plants that will look good together. You will be better able to avoid ending up with a few of this color and a few of that, and multicolored assortments of several different kinds of flowers.

This isn't to say that you should not plan a multicolored garden if you really want one. Some gardeners love a lively assortment of bright hues that is particularly easy to achieve with annuals in mixed-color assortments. Most garden centers offer mixed-color packs of snapdragons, petunias, impatiens, celosia, zinnias, and other favorite flowers; in fact, single-color packs of plants other than impatiens, marigolds, and petunias can be hard to find in some places. So if you want a brilliant mix of colors, go for it. Just be sure it's what you really want.

I must confess that I number myself among those gardeners who find polychromatic gardens jarring and discordant, for the most part. It's simply too much color for me, visually overwhelming. After a few weeks you, too, might find so much bright color rather chaotic, and you may find that you are simply tired of looking at it. The problem is most acute with annuals, most of which bloom throughout a good portion of the summer.

If you are not sure what sort of color scheme would best please you in your garden, start with a simple blend and add to it in subsequent years if you feel you need more color. It is easier and more satisfying to add than to subtract color.

Here are some guidelines to use, and some issues to ponder, to help you plan a color scheme for your garden.

First, think about the basic kinds of colors you like in other areas of your life—your home and its furnishings, your clothes and accessories. Do you generally prefer bright, warm colors (reds, oranges, and yellows) or cool, peaceful colors (blues, greens, and violets)? Are you drawn to subtle, harmonious blends of colors, or to contrasting colors? Rich, deep tones or pale pastels? Do you like the serenity and cleanness of white instead of other colors?

Very basically, there are four ways to work with color in the garden. You can combine harmonious or analogous colors, or contrasting or complementary colors, you can rely on a single flower color contrasted against green foliage, or you can plant in an assortment of mixed colors.

Sample Color Schemes

Harmonious Schemes

rose-pink, lavender, purple
pink, blue, purple
red, rose, pink
red, scarlet, gold
red, orange, yellow
scarlet, yellow-orange, yellow
deep red, pink, lavender
warm pink, orange, gold, cream
rose, pink, blue
salmon, orange, yellow
red and pink
pink and purple
pink and blue

Contrasting Schemes

blue and orange; add yellow if you like
blue-violet, salmon, apricot
red-violet flowers with yellow-green foliage
red, yellow, blue
red, white, blue
pink, light blue, orange
lavender and clear yellow
peach and lavender
purple and cream
purple and gold
yellow and white
pink and yellow; add purple if you like
red and purple
blue and yellow
violet and pale yellow
magenta and orange (whew!)

Harmonious Color Schemes

Harmonious, or analogous, colors are related; they are located near one another on an artist's color wheel, and blend smoothly with one another. Examples of harmonious color schemes are red, orange, and gold, or blue, purple, and pink. Analogous color schemes are often quiet and subtle, as in the case of a blend of pastel shades of pink, rose, and lilac petunias. But they can also be surprisingly dramatic, as in the case of a bed of chrysanthemums in brilliant gold, rich orange, russet, and crimson. These combinations of closely related colors are most appealing to the eyes of some people. For others, contrast is needed to bring more life to the composition.

An easy way to get a harmonious combination of colors is to plant several varieties of one type—or better yet, one species—of flower. You might want to plant several kinds of celosia, for example, or chrysanthemums, or pansies. The colors of the different cultivars may be different in hue and intensity, but they will almost always harmonize with one another. Individual cultivars within a hybrid series, such as Dazzler hybrid impatiens, Flair petunias, or Rocket snapdragons, are especially compatible.

Contrasting Color Schemes

Contrasting colors are farther apart on a color wheel and placing them next to each other emphasizes their different qualities. Complementary colors lie opposite one another on the color wheel, and contrast more intensely than any other juxtaposition of colors. Examples of complementary colors include blue and orange, purple and yellow, and red and green. Complementary colors placed next to one another tend to intensify both colors. The nineteenth century English landscape painter John Constable placed small strokes of red amid expanses of foliage in his paintings to make the greens look greener. If you look closely you may perceive the same effect in a garden.

If you want to plant a garden of complementary colors, you will probably find the most pleasing results by planting the softer of the two colors over a larger portion of the garden and using the brighter color sparingly, as an accent. For example, if you want to combine blue salvia with orange marigolds, plant lots more salvia than marigolds. If you plant more marigolds and fewer salvia, the orange will overwhelm the blue.

Another way to tone down a contrasting scheme is to soften the shade of the brighter color. Instead of using orange marigolds with the salvia, you could instead plant salmon-colored geraniums or petunias.

A third way to soften intensely contrasting colors is to introduce some neutral tones—white flowers or silver foliage—to blend the colors, or to surround the contrasting hues with lots of green foliage to absorb some of the color.

Contrasting color schemes can be quite beautiful, but you may find you like them best in a garden that will be viewed from a distance—from across the lawn, perhaps—rather than up close, such as in a container garden on a patio.

Single-Color Gardens

The simplest color scheme of all is built on a single color, perhaps expressed in several different shades and tints, and perhaps with a small amount of a second color added as an accent. Monochromatic gardens can be quite soothing to the eye, and their simplicity can work extremely well in a formal setting. You might like a garden of all white flowers, or red, or yellow. Or you could combine several shades of pink.

Single-color gardens need not be boring, either. You can vary the types of flowers, plant heights, shapes, and textures, flower sizes, and tones of color (pale, bright, or dark). Or you can mix in some plants with variegated or colored foliage for added interest.

Multicolored Gardens

In a mixed color, or polychromatic, garden, the variety of colors included depends entirely on the gardener's preference. Multicolored gardens can be blindingly brilliant, if all strong colors are used, or they can be cheerful and festive, if you mix pastels and soft shades. You can create a multicolor garden by planting a favorite flower in mixed colors, or by planting a selection of plants, each in a different color, for a rainbow of blossoms.

A polychromatic garden generally works best if one color is dominant, to bring a sense of cohesiveness to the overall scheme. And don't spread the plants of each color throughout the garden like so many polka dots; you will lose the visual impact, and your garden will look more like a motley collection of plants. Instead, plant in color groups, in bands or drifts or clumps. Don't plant one yellow marigold, plant five or nine or nineteen.

To get the best effect from a polychromatic garden, surround it with lots of green to provide some visual relief, and give the viewer's eye some rest. Set your flowers of many colors in front of evergreens, or a hedge, or in a bed in the middle of a lawn.

Other Design Considerations

Flower color is not the only criterion to use in choosing plants for the garden. Their height,

size and shape, and texture are also important. Creating a first-rate garden is rather like composing a painting, or a piece of music—in order to make a unified whole, all the parts must fit together in a way that is both comfortable and interesting.

In order to allow all the plants in the garden to be visible, as well as to create a pleasing visual depth, you should grow plants of several different heights. It may help to imagine the garden as a painting or photograph, with the space divided into a foreground, middle ground, and background. In a border or bed that will be viewed primarily from one side, the background plants are farthest from the viewer, and should be the tallest plants in the garden, so they will not be blocked by the plants in front of them. Plant successively smaller plants as you work toward the front of the garden, with the lowest plants along the front edge.

Plant heights are relative, and a plant that belongs in the middle ground of a small garden may work in the front of a garden of large plants. But as a general rule of thumb, we will in this book consider plants over three feet tall to work best as background plants, plants from one and one-half to three feet to belong in the middle ground, and plants under one and one-half feet to be used in the front of the garden or as edging.

In an island bed that will be viewed from all sides, the tallest plants go in the center of the garden and the smallest plants around the outer edges. Good background or center-of-the-island candidates include tall, upright plants like hollyhocks, gladiolus, daylilies, cosmos, cleome, and sunflowers. Climbing vines such as morning glory or honeysuckle or climbing roses can be trained on trellises or other supports to work as background plants. Or shrubs can form the backdrop of the garden. The table, Background Plants, in the Appendix, provides a list of readily available tall and climbing plants, for easy reference.

If the garden will be devoted to sun-loving species, it should ideally be positioned with the long axis running east to west, and the front of the garden facing south. Such an orientation will mean the tallest plants will be on the north side of the garden where they will not cast shade on their lower growing neighbors. If you cannot site your garden this way, don't worry about it. Your plants should still perform adequately—most will adapt to less-than-perfect conditions. If you are concerned that tall plants will cast too much shade, choose plants that can tolerate partial shade to plant in front of them (see the list of Plants for Shade, in the Appendix).

Design Hints

- ✪ Keep the planting in scale with the site. A huge garden will overwhelm a small yard, and conversely, a small garden will have little visual impact in an expansive lawn.
- ✪ Make your first garden small and simple, concentrating on just a few types of plants in an uncomplicated color scheme repeated throughout the garden.
- ✪ Follow your instincts—don't be afraid to break the rules if you don't like them.
- ✪ Choose plants that will give you a gradation of heights from the front to the back of the garden (or outer edge to center of an island bed). But let a few plants drift over the boundaries of their groups for a softer, more integrated look.

- ✪ Plant flowers to create drifts of color; do not dot individual plants about the garden, and do not plant in straight rows unless you are using them to create a particular pattern. Even in a small garden, try to plant at least three of the same plant together in a clump for good visual effect.
- ✪ Use a variety of plant forms and flower shapes to keep the garden interesting: round, clustered flowers; flat, daisylike flowers; trumpet- and bell-shaped blossoms; tall vertical spires and spikes; branching flowers. (Chapter Five provides information on the forms and flower shapes of specific plants.)

The middle ground of the garden holds medium-size plants. Many of these are bushy, and their foliage adds masses of greenery to the garden when the plants are not blooming. Some plants for the middle ground are hardy aster, China aster, columbine, coralbells, calendula, snapdragon, celosia, nicotiana, foxglove, salvia, African marigold, zinnia, iris, campanula, beebalm, veronica, false dragonhead, coreopsis, rudbeckia (which could serve as a background plant in a garden of small plants), achillea, astilbe, hardy geranium, hosta, chrysanthemum, and Autumn Joy sedum. See the table, Plants for the Middle Ground, in the Appendix, for a more extensive list.

In the foreground of the garden picture go the compact plants, with the very smallest going along the outer edges of the bed, border, or container. Choose your foreground plants to be in scale with the other plants in the garden. A plant that may work in the front of a large garden of big plants would overwhelm a composition of smaller plants. A sense of scale is important in creating a pleasing garden picture, so always consider the mature height of the plants you want to grow. Some good low-growing and edging plants are dianthus, sweet alyssum, curly parsley, lilyturf, pansy (in cool weather), evergreen candytuft, lady's mantle, thyme, sanvitalia or creeping zinnia, dwarf marigold, wax begonia, impatiens, lobelia, petunia, ageratum, portulaca, annual phlox, nasturtium, verbena, torenia, and dwarf zinnia. See the Appendix for a list of plants to use as edging and in the front of the garden.

To make it easier to care for your garden, you can group plants according to their maintenance needs. Plant together flowers that need to be watered frequently, or those that can tolerate drier soil. Group plants that need especially rich soil, and work extra organic matter and fertilizers into the soil in that part of the garden. If you are growing both annuals and perennials, you might want to plant all the annuals together to make it easier to clean up the garden at the end of the growing season.

If you want to have flowers from spring through fall, choose plants that bloom in each season. Plant species and cultivars with different blooming times. Some widely hybridized flowers, such as daylilies, iris, and lilies, can be had in cultivars that bloom early, midseason, and late in the daylily or iris or lily blooming period. Planting some of each type will give you flowers over the longest possible time.

Relative blooming times are not usually given on the plant labels at local nurseries; unless the staff is especially knowledgeable about the cultivars they sell, you may find it difficult to choose varieties that will provide a succession of bloom. But the catalogs of the better mail-order nurseries do contain this information. You might be able to scout out which daylilies or iris or lilies are for sale locally, then go home and look them up in your catalogs (or a friend's catalogs) to find out if they flower early, late, or midseason.

Many annuals will bloom all summer long if you deadhead them regularly to keep the plants from setting seeds. Marigolds, annual salvia, verbena, nicotiana, and geraniums are just a few of the plants that behave this way. Others, such as snapdragon, will rebloom if you cut them back after the first flowering is over. Some perennials, such as nepeta and perennial salvia, will also rebloom, in a smaller way, if cut back after they flower.

Considering the form and texture of the plants themselves, as well as the flowers, will add an extra dimension to the garden. There are flowers with round, flat, daisylike shapes, cups, bells, and trumpets, spiky vertical forms, fluffy plumes like astilbe and some celosia, and tiny, delicate blossoms like baby's breath and forget-me-nots. Plants may have bold, sculptural leaves like brunnera, angular, sword-shaped leaves like those of iris and gladiolus, delicate, ferny foliage such as that of astilbe and bleeding heart, or glossy leaves like English ivy. You could choose cultivars of some plants that have golden, purple, or variegated (patterned) leaves.

Foliage is especially important in a perennial garden, where individual plants are only in bloom for a limited number of days or weeks—the rest of the time they are simply clumps of greenery. A combination of forms and textures makes the garden interesting. It may seem an overwhelming challenge at first, but as you gain experience with more plants you will develop an awareness of their form and texture. In the meantime, consult the plant profiles in Chapter Five for guidance.

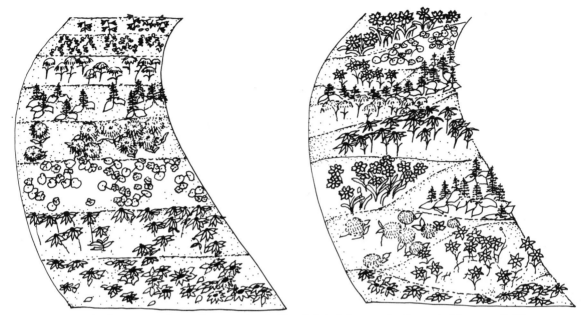

For a naturalistic look, plant flowers in drifts (right) instead of straight rows (left).

Plant Placement in the Garden

If a naturalistic look is what you're after, don't line up plants in rows like little soldiers. Instead, plant them in clumps if the garden is small, or flowing, curved drifts if the garden is large. Let a few plants from adjoining drifts intermingle along the borders to avoid creating a hard edge. Conventional wisdom has it that it is easier to create an informal, natural look with an odd number of plants in each clump; even numbers tend to make us create symmetrical patterns that don't look natural in the garden. Instead of planting a clump of four plants, plant five, or seven, or eleven.

You will probably find it easiest to position the tallest plants first. In a container or an island bed that will be viewed from all sides, the tallest plants go in the center. In a windowbox or bed that will be viewed primarily from one side, place the tallest plants in the back of the garden. Position the remaining plants in descending order of size, finishing with the smallest plants in the front or around the outer edges of the garden.

If you are creating the garden with plants in individual pots, rather than flats or cell packs, you can set the plants, still in their containers, where you expect to plant them. Step back and look over the prospective garden to see if you like the arrangement. If you're not satisfied, you can easily move the plants around to redesign the garden before digging a single hole.

Special Effects

Here are a few tricks you can use to achieve some dramatic effects in your garden.

As you begin to plan the garden, think about what you want to feature most prominently in the landscape, which plants or landscape features you want visitors to notice first.

If your house dominates the scene, make the gardens simple, with flowers in a monochromatic color scheme that complements the color and style of the house. On the other hand, if you want the garden to be the focal point of the landscape, use bright colors in harmonious or contrasting combinations, according to the look you prefer.

For a formal look, plan a garden in a neat, straight-edged geometric shape—square or rectangular or triangular, perhaps. Grow tidy, well-shaped plants and keep them carefully groomed, and use a simple color scheme—all white, red and white, or blue and white are some good possibilities. Traditionally, the flowers considered most appropriate for a formal garden have been classic florist flowers. Lilies, iris, poppies, roses, phlox, and tulips are some good choices for formal beds and borders.

To achieve a romantic feeling, use lots of flowers with an open, flowing growth habit, old-fashioned flowers, and fragrant blossoms in a mix of soft colors. Trailing vines whose tendrils arc into space, climb up trellises, and ramble across the ground add to the romantic appeal. Cottage garden favorites such as hollyhock, campanula, dianthus, daisies, verbena, forget-me-not, pansy, and morning glories are all wonderfully romantic.

If a bold, contemporary look is what you're after, opt for large-leaved plants with simple, interesting lines. Cacti and succulents are ideal in southwestern gardens, and big tropical foliage does the job in the South. In cooler climes, ornamental grasses can create a contemporary, sculptural effect, as can hardy varieties of yucca and opuntia (prickly pear), or bold-leaved cannas grown as annuals.

To spotlight a favorite type of plant, grow it in a knockout color and surround it with a sea of green.

If you want to draw attention to a fountain, piece of sculpture, sundial, or other ornament, place it in the center of two axes that converge in the middle of the garden. Plant flowers along the axes to create a trail of color for the eye to follow toward the special object in the center of the garden.

Areas shaded by trees sometimes tend to disappear because they are too dim to be noticeable. To keep a dark spot a visible, active part of the landscape, plant white or pastel colored flowers to light up the shadows.

To make a small garden seem bigger it is essential to plant in a gradation of heights to create some visual depth. Also, plant warm-colored flowers up front and cool colors farther back. Warm colors appear to come forward visually, while cool colors recede. You can use this optical illusion to help create a feeling of greater depth and space. Another way to gain optical space is to create multiple garden levels with terraced beds, instead of planting the entire garden on a single plane. The terraced garden will seem larger than a flat, unbroken space.

For a really simple but elegant garden, you might consider planting only bearded iris or peonies. Both plants are quite handsome planted by themselves in a border, and a planting of either is a lovely way to divide space in the yard. Peonies are also extremely easy to care for, and their foliage is attractive all season. Lilies, too, can be featured in a garden of their own. Masses of daylilies in several colors make a pretty, low-maintenance border along a driveway or sidewalk.

Special Considerations for Designing Container Gardens

Plants in pots add a touch of charm to your surroundings, whether or not you also have a garden in the ground. To get the best effect from your potted plants, instead of just plunking pots of plants randomly about the premises, think of all those contained plants as the parts of a garden, and plan them so they all unite into a coherent whole. You can use the same guidelines to plan the container garden that you would use to plan a garden bed or border in the ground. The difference is that the container garden is executed on a smaller scale, and the plants are separated by their containers, making each individual plant seem more important.

A well-designed container garden, whether it consists of lots of different pots, or several plants growing together in a single large container, will have plants in a gradation of heights, an assortment of compatible shapes and textures, and a thoughtfully chosen range of colors. It is generally best to keep the color scheme simple, because all the containers already make the garden look rather busy. If you want to plant a multicolored container garden, put all the plants in pots of a single neutral color (white, or dark green or brown, for instance). On the other hand, if you have a collection of interesting, unusual containers, plant all-white or monochromatic flowers that will show off the pots. Trailing plants that cascade over the edges of pots soften the look of containers and add to the appeal of the garden.

Treat a large freestanding container that will be viewed from all sides like a miniature version of an island bed. Place the tallest plants in the center of the container and the shortest plants around the outer edges. When planting a windowbox or other container that will be viewed from one side, put the tall plants at the back and the shorter plants toward the front.

A container garden can be as simple as a half-barrel planted with geraniums in the center, surrounded by dusty miller, with lobelia or sweet alyssum as edging and variegated vinca trailing over the sides. Or it might be a series of pots placed on the front porch steps, with several more containers grouped by the door. Apartment dwellers might fasten pots of flowers to the railing of an outdoor balcony or fire escape. You can group small plants in windowboxes, and individually potted specimens in a rectangular planter box or Victorian fernery. Camouflage the tops of the pots in a group planter with sphagnum moss.

Make a Plant List

When you have gotten a reasonably good idea of the sort of growing conditions you have to offer plants, the colors you are looking for, and the size you want the garden to be, you can start making a list of the plants you want to buy. Use the information in Chapter Five and the Appendix for guidance. Even if your garden will be small, and you think you can keep all the plant names in your head, it is best to make a list. If you don't it is all too easy to get confused or forget something when you go to the garden center.

Plant Selection Guide

Here's a summary of things to consider when determining whether or not a plant is right for your garden:

1. Does it need full sun, partial shade, or shade?

2. What color are its flowers (or leaves, if it is a foliage plant)? What "temperature" is the color (warm pink or cool pink, for instance)? Will the color fit your color scheme?

Designing the Garden / 45

3. How tall will the plant be when mature? Does it belong in the foreground, middle ground, or background of the garden?

4. Will its form and texture work well with other plants in the garden? Aim for a combination of plant forms (spiky, bushy, moundlike) and an assortment of different foliage shapes and textures (smooth and narrow, toothed and oval, lacy and delicate). See Chapter Five for information on the design qualities of individual plants.

5. What are the plant's needs for soil and moisture?
   - Well-drained but moist, well-drained and rather dry, or constantly moist?
   - Rich or average fertility? Can it tolerate poor soil?
   - Any special pH needs?

6. Does the plant have special characteristics that are important?
   - Good for cutting
   - Suitable for windowboxes and pots
   - Hanging basket plant
   - Low maintenance needs
   - Fragrant flowers
   - Tolerates drought

If you still prefer to let your plant choices be spontaneous instead of picking plants from the descriptions in this or other books, at least make a list of the *kinds* of plants you want (such as tall pink flowers for the back of the bed). Then read the plant labels at the nursery to find plants that meet your needs.

If you find yourself enjoying the process of working out a plant list, you can go a step farther and note on your garden map where each type of plant will go. Pencil in areas for each plant on your garden sketch.

Time for a Reality Check

Before you rush off to buy all those plants for your garden-to-be, take just a few moments to run a reality check on your plans. Do you think you will have the time and energy needed to maintain this garden after it is planted? If not, scale it down a bit. You can always expand next year.

Are all the plants you have chosen likely to thrive in the microclimate of your garden? If your garden will be shady, make sure your plant list does not contain any sunlovers. Consider plant hardiness, too. If your garden site is exposed to cold winter winds, or located at the bottom of a hill where cold air will collect, your growing conditions may actually be equivalent to those of a zone farther north.

Pocket gardens of nasturtiums and coreopsis.

Morning glories can dress up a mailbox.

Although you live in zone 6, for instance, conditions in your garden may be more like those in zone 5. Perennial plants of borderline hardiness in the rest of your geographic area might not survive in your particular garden.

If you are relatively new to gardening, it is better to choose plants conservatively until you gain more experience, in order to avoid disappointments. Concentrate on easy-to-grow plants for the first few years and your garden is bound to succeed. A list of plants that are adaptable, durable, and generally easy to grow can be found in the Appendix.

A Compendium of Design Ideas

Even the most ordinary plants can be effective if you use them creatively. Here are some ideas for using everyday plants in engaging—and in some cases, amusing—ways.

To Welcome You Home

Put a pocket garden at the entrance to the driveway. For a sunny, hot color scheme you might plant nasturtiums or zinnias backed by coreopsis. Or you could try a softer combination of sweet alyssum in front, backed by petunias in rose, pink, and lavender, with white snapdragons or nicotiana in back.

Group plants around a lamppost at the end of the sidewalk or path leading to the house. Put dianthus or pink petunias in front, with campanula, lisianthus, or balloon flower behind them. For added interest, train morning glory vines around the lamppost.

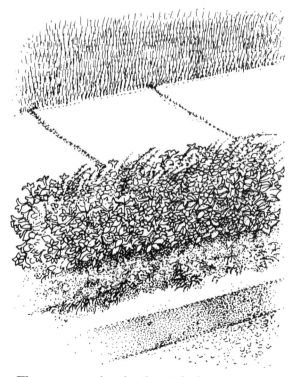

Flowers growing in the strip between sidewalk and curb beautify the neighborhood.

If you have a mailbox out by the street, you can give it some real charm by training morning glories to climb the post and tumble over the top of the box. Just make sure the vines don't obscure your name or house number or interfere with the opening of the mailbox. You can also buy a special type of wooden planter that fits over the mailbox, and fill it with sweet alyssum, begonias, lobelia, torenia, or other small plants.

Dress up the front porch by suspending hanging baskets of vines above windowboxes fastened to the porch railing. For a sunny porch, try trailing nasturtiums in the baskets and basil or oregano, marigolds, and sweet alyssum (back to front) in the windowboxes. In a partly shaded spot, fuchsias, ivy or vinca can dangle from the hanging baskets, and China asters, torenia, and lobelia can grow in the boxes below. The plants will afford some privacy, and help turn the porch into an inviting and comfortable place to sit.

To bring some carefree color to a shaded sidewalk or path leading to your door, try planting banks of impatiens, coleus, and ferns alongside the walkway. Choose white or an orangey shade of impatiens instead of cool pinks or lavenders to harmonize with the coleus. None of these plants needs much in the way of maintenance except for some water during spells of dry weather.

Give a gift to the neighborhood by planting flowers in tree lawns and the grassy strip between the sidewalk and the curb. Impatiens are great for massing under trees. For the strip garden, you could try nepeta in the center, surrounded by white nicotiana and edged with sweet alyssum. Celosia would also work in the center if you want hotter, brighter colors and do not have to deal with any shade.

A row of peonies along a driveway makes a grand entrance, especially when the plants are in bloom.

If you have a sunny slope in front of the house, for a change from the typical lawn (which is difficult to mow on a hill, anyway) consider planting a carpet of moss pinks, *Phlox subulata,* in drifts, clumps, or ribbons of color. In spring the slope will be a mass of pink, lavender, rose, and white. For a longer-lasting but less dramatic display, substitute vinca (also called periwinkle or myrtle). The plants produce pretty blue-violet flowers in spring and early summer, and their glossy leaves remain attractive all season; in some climates they are evergreen.

To make a grand entrance, plant masses of daylilies along the driveway. For a more formal look, you could plant peonies instead. If a natural, meadowy feeling is more to your taste, line the drive with ornamental grasses.

Paths and Pavings

To soften the look of a path, tuck small plants among the paving stones. In a shady spot you might try violets or torenia. In the sun, use creeping thyme or another kind of thyme, or a small dianthus.

If you have a path made of bricks set in sand, you can achieve a similar effect by removing some of the bricks, filling the holes with good garden soil, and planting in the small pockets. Portulaca in mixed colors would be pretty in a sunny location; very small hostas are interesting in the shade.

If you have a path or patio made of bricks or pavers set in sand, you can create a garden in it. Remove some of the bricks or stones, scoop out the sand, and fill the holes with good garden soil or potting mix. Plant herbs or small flowers in the pockets of soil.

Even a tiny front yard can become a garden spot, with scaled-down borders of small plants.

You can also use the same idea for a brick or stone patio. Put small herbs or flowers in the holes.

Pockets and Small Spaces

Here's an idea for a tiny front yard, to create an especially enticing entrance for a country cottage or bungalow. First, surround the yard with a classic white picket fence. Put garden borders all along the inside of the fence (the smaller the yard, the smaller the borders, and the flowers planted in them, should be). Carve out a small island bed in the center of the lawn. You will wind up with lots of color and less lawn to mow.

To welcome spring, tuck a pocket of pansies into a secret spot—next to a shrub, around the curve of a path, on the south side of a boulder.

To bridge the transition between sun and shade, here's an idea for a small bed to put in the borderline area. This garden will work best where the shade is fairly light, such as would be cast by a tall tree with a high, lacy canopy. Plant pink and purple columbines, or a hybrid strain such as McKana Giant or Songbird in mixed colors, in the back of the bed, along the edge of the shade. Plant pink petunias in the middle of the bed, in the sunshine, and an edging of sweet alyssum in the front. Or plant a mass of impatiens, which can grow in both sun and shade.

Delightful little pocket gardens can be created from just a few plants and tucked into any small vacant spot. You might, for example, start with a small ornamental grass, such as pennisetum, in the back of the garden, with some brunnera and a few clumps of chives, and an edging of small dianthus.

Carpets, Geometry, and Crazy Shapes

For a blast of hot color in a sunny spot, how about making a simple carpet bed: fill a rectangular bed with magenta impatiens or celosia, intersperse some clumps of golden yellow French marigolds or small coreopsis, and outline the whole with dusty miller.

If you want to try a formal geometric bed, consider this scheme in blue and gold: bisect a small square bed with two diagonal axes that meet in a central circle. Plant purple or blue pansies or violas along the axes, and tall yellow

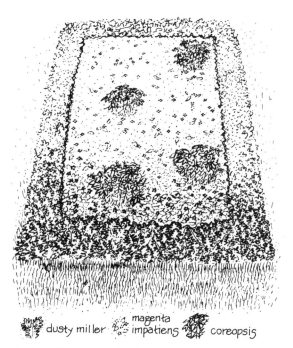

dusty miller   magenta impatiens   coreopsis

A simple carpet bed.

A pocket of plants for the smallest of gardens.

and orange marigolds in the central area. Fill the four triangular areas created by the axes with yellow French marigolds, and edge the bed with ageratum.

Or maybe you would prefer a circular variation in pink and blue. Bisect a circular bed with two perpendicular axes, again intersecting in a circle in the center of the bed. Plant a blue salvia, such as Victoria, in the center circle, pink petunias or zinnias in the wedge-shaped areas, and blue lobelia or ageratum in the axes and outer ring.

Take off on a formal French parterre by creating your own miniature version with pansies and parsley. Make one or more small rectangular beds and plant them with pansies in mixed colors, or impatiens, begonias, portulaca, or other small plants of your choice. Edge each bed with curly parsley, to take the

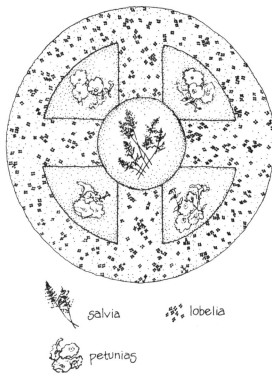

salvia   lobelia

petunias

A circular bed of salvia, petunias, and lobelia.

place of the boxwood used to edge the elaborate parterres in the grand manor gardens of Europe.

If you are a diehard romantic, plant your valentine a heart-shaped bed of lavender carpeted with sweet alyssum, with dianthus or pink begonias around the edges.

On a somewhat more practical note, herb gardens lend themselves readily to geometric shapes. One attractive configuration is a sort of wagon wheel approach with a circular garden divided into wedges, each of which is planted with a different herb. Or you could divide a square garden into blocks like a checkerboard, and plant in the blocks. Remember, though, that if the square is of any appreciable size,

you will need to leave some blocks empty so you that you will be able to step into the garden to weed and harvest. Fill the empty blocks with an attractive mulch or groundcover; creeping thyme would be one appropriate choice.

Circles, Ovals, and Soft Edges
Flowing curves are the most appealing shapes for many gardeners. I like loose, rounded forms in my own gardens, and find them easier to work with than more precise shapes. Here are some ways to work common plants into these soft forms.

Mass annuals in drifts to mimic the look of a perennial border. To create a garden with a background of tall flowers, you could use cleome, cosmos, hollyhocks, gladiolus, or sunflowers. In the middle ground try

A miniature parterre of pansies and parsley.

A small bed of blue salvia, petunias, candytuft, begonias, and fragrant thyme.

nicotiana, poppies, snapdragons, and/or salvia, with dwarf zinnias or marigolds in the foreground.

In a circular island bed, you could mix clumps of purple and white iris with pink snapdragons, pink dianthus, and blue lobelia.

A pretty oval bed could combine peonies, irises, and Iceland poppies for a symphony of color in early summer.

A simple scheme for a small bed that is easy to expand to fill a larger space mixes a background planting of blue salvia with drifts of pink petunias and lavender globe candytuft, white begonias, or dwarf dahlias or snapdragons, and thyme in front.

If you love a particular flower, such as iris, daylily, zinnia, or impatiens, for example, and want to grow lots of it, you might want to plant an entire bed of the flower in different shades, arranged in curved wide rows to create the effect of ribbons of color.

A gardener with a sense of humor might enjoy a wacky spiral-patterned garden of deep rose impatiens or red begonias swirled around the same flowers in a lighter shade of pink.

Ideas for Containers

Plants in containers can create a feeling of unity between garden and house. Choose potted plants for decks and patios in colors that echo the colors in your garden, to create a visual link.

Potted petunias, dianthus, marigolds, zinnias, salvia, and phlox can be grouped to decorate outdoor living spaces: patio benches, picnic tables, the pavement around a swimming pool, and a low retaining wall around a patio are some likely places to set containers full of flowers.

On a sunny deck or patio, the following combination will work in large tubs or big rectangular planter boxes. Put blue salvia in the

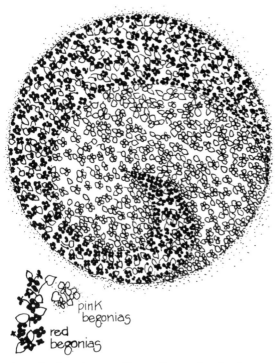

pink begonias

red begonias

A spiral pattern of wax begonias in two colors.

Create a lavish tub garden with geraniums, dusty miller, lobelia, and variegated vinca.

center; surround it with salmon or rose-pink geraniums (use a group of three in a tub) and dusty miller, and edge with lavender verbena or blue lobelia. In a freestanding rectangular box that can be viewed from all sides, plant the salvia down the center, with geraniums and dusty miller along both sides of the salvia, and the verbena or lobelia along the edges of the box. For added charm in tub or box, intersperse some trailing variegated vinca with the edging plants.

A simpler variation might surround a central clump of the salvia with pale yellow petunias and an edging of luminous blue lobelia.

For a rosy theme, group pink cleome or tall pink snapdragons in the center of a tub, surround the tall plants with petunias in a rich rose-pink shade, and edge with sweet alyssum.

In honor of the summer solstice, you could fill a tub or planter box with this sunny combination: coreopsis in the center, next, a ring of orange marigolds, then yellow French marigolds around the outside, finishing with an edging of sanvitalia.

If you love cut flowers, you might like to plant a sort of living bouquet in a big container. Just choose a compatible assortment of flowers suitable for cutting. Here are two examples: Surround a central group of blue salvia with verbena and China asters, and edge with vinca or sweet alyssum. Or plant cleome or snapdragons in the middle, surrounding them with nicotiana and globe candytuft.

A lovely grouping for a large windowbox or planter combines blue salvia for height with rose and lavender verbena (the low, sprawling type will arc off into space in a delightful way) and dusty miller, with variegated vinca spilling over the edges of the box. In a location in partial shade, you can replace the verbena with torenia in an assortment of purple, pink, and white shades.

To make effective use of smaller containers, try grouping several pots, each planted with a single type of flower, or just a couple of different plants. Red and white nicotiana is one possibility, or nasturtiums in mixed colors, scarlet salvia with creamy zinnias or white marguerite daisies, or marigolds and zinnias in yellow, gold, cream, and white. If you like petunias, group pots of pink, purple, and white petunias edged with sweet alyssum in white or purple.

To celebrate spring, fill a strawberry jar with pansies and set it by the front or back door, or on a deck or patio where it will be readily visible from inside the house. For summer, plant pale pink nicotiana in the top of the jar, and purple sweet alyssum in the little side pockets.

Plant containers for a shady spot with impatiens in vibrant rose or pastel pink and lavender, with a small-leaved ivy trailing over the edge of the pot.

To achieve a massed effect, place pots of nasturtiums on a tiered stand or shelving, and let the trailing plants tumble all together. A similar effect can be achieved with ivy geraniums or other cascading geranium hybrids. I have also seen a column of geraniums created by planting them in half-pots mounted one above the other on a wall. These pots look like hanging baskets cut in half, and are specifically designed to be mounted on walls and fences.

Another idea for using individual pots is to line up a row of potted plants on top of a

Individual pots of nasturtiums placed on a tiered stand create a mass of blossoms.

A strawberry jar full of pansies for spring.

retaining wall to soften the severe line of the wall. Cascading plants are especially pretty; try a row of fuchsias in a shady location.

Gardens for Shade

Although a location in full sun affords the widest choice of design possibilities, there are plenty of options for shade gardeners, as well. Here are a few ideas to get you started.

You can make a pretty, semicircular garden for a shady spot by combining a background of fluffy astilbe in shades of red, pink, and white with a middle ground of bleeding heart and columbines, fronted by impatiens or small hostas. If you like, create a transition between lawn and garden with a patch of vinca rambling about in front of the flowers.

Create a tiny jewel of a shade garden from ferns and astilbe, with torenia in front, and maybe some ivy, vinca, or pachysandra as a cool, green groundcover. A metal edging strip sunk into the ground between the groundcover and the garden will help to keep the spreading groundcover plants from invading the flower bed.

If pink and blue appeal to you, plant a backdrop of pink astilbe, a middle ground of the blue forget-me-nots of myosotis or brunnera, with lobelia or violets as edging, or ajuga as a groundcover.

An easy-care foliage composition can be created with drifts of hosta and coleus in assorted colors and patterns. If you prefer a bolder look, mix in some caladiums.

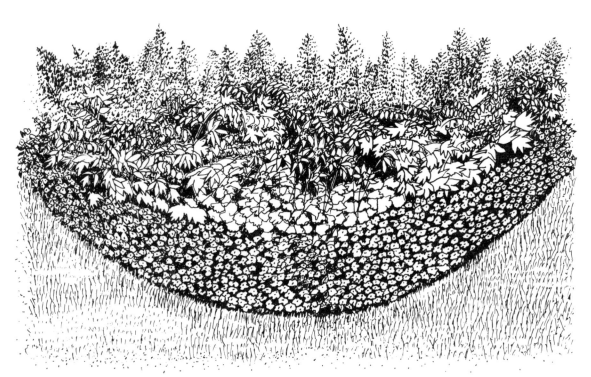

A half-moon garden for shade: astilbe, bleeding heart, columbines, and impatiens.

Drifts of hosta and coleus, along with caladiums, add up to a low-maintenance shade garden.

For a serene, restful, green and white garden, combine the large leaves of white-variegated caladium with ferns, small hostas, white impatiens, and a groundcover of lamium (particularly the cultivar White Nancy, if you can find it locally). Or substitute white lobelia for the lamium.

Here's a cool green oasis that's perfect for the shady corner of a patio: install a lattice screen, and train ivy to climb it. Plant the ivy in planter boxes or a small bed at the edge of the patio. In front of the screen, place a small statue, fountain, or other ornament to serve as a focal point, or a small bench to sit on. Group pots of ferns and caladiums around the bench or ornament. If you choose to create this calm retreat in a corner of the garden instead of on a

patio, plant vinca or another groundcover under the bench and around the plants and ornament, and plant the ferns and caladiums directly in the ground.

Borders and Dividers

In addition to serving as decoration, plants can help to define and separate different areas of a yard or landscape. Here are some suggestions for ways to use plants as borders and dividers.

Peonies and irises can make a lovely border that is full of color in late spring. Including several types of bearded iris with different blooming times, along with Siberian iris, which flowers a bit later, will extend the season of color in this border. The leaves of the peonies will remain handsome all summer, even when

A leafy, cool oasis makes the patio an ideal retreat on a hot summer day.

the plants are not in bloom, and the addition of a groundcover enhances the effect. To make the border, plant peonies in a row, and plant irises along both sides of the peonies. Finally, plant a groundcover such as vinca among and between them.

A row of giant sunflowers can also serve as a rather fanciful divider, and in fall you can collect and roast the seeds, or leave the seedheads in place for birds to enjoy. Tall hollyhocks also make a pretty screen.

Flowers can effectively soften the look of a fence, screen, or wall, and these structures, in turn, provide an attractive backdrop for the blossoms. For a pretty pink and blue bed with a cottage garden look, plant morning glories to climb a fence or lattice screen, or train them on a trellis, with a blue salvia such as Victoria in front, and drifts of pink, rose, and pale salmon zinnias or geraniums among and in front of the salvia. Finish with an edging of blue lobelia or ageratum.

An easy-care combination to front a classic picket fence combines pink peonies with clematis in purple, violet, pink, red, or white trained on the fence.

Whimsy and Fantasy

Here are a few ways to have fun with a flower garden and create some unusual, interesting effects.

You can plant masses of baby's breath for a romantic, cloudlike look in midsummer. A narrow bed of baby's breath planted some

Giant sunflowers create a screen.

distance in front of a flower garden will create a light screen or scrim when in bloom, through which to view the flowers beyond—an intriguing visual effect.

For another unusual look, you could throw out the rules of garden design and create a millefleurs garden, a small, sunny bed of mixed flowers in assorted colors. Instead of planting each type of flower in a clump, set out plants individually for a sort of pointillist effect. Plant sweet alyssum among the flowers to create a ground for them. Although this kind of approach flies in the face of generally accepted principles of good garden design (including those set forth earlier in this chapter), it can be fun.

You might instead let your garden be inspired by art, and copy a garden from a favorite painting. The great impressionist Claude Monet did many lovely paintings of his marvellous gardens at Giverny with which many of us are familiar, but gardens and plants have stimulated the work of many artists in many eras.

Everyone loves a grape arbor, but they take time to establish. Here is a way to create a shady bower in a single growing season. Plant lots of morning glories to cover an arbor and shade a picnic table, or to train around the roof and supports of a porch to frame the view with flowers. I trained a combination of morning glories and moonflowers around the porch of a small cottage my husband and I rented some years ago, and the effect was almost magical. The sky blue morning glories opened with the dawn and held sway throughout the day. In late afternoon they were joined by the sweet-scented moonflowers. At sundown the morning glories closed and the pearly white moonflowers continued blooming to rule the porch all night.

Color Themes

Finally, to wrap up this collection of design ideas, here are some options for gardens in a variety of color schemes.

One soft, cool combination is a blend of phlox, verbena, violas, petunias, snapdragons, ageratum, and sweet alyssum in lavender, purple, pink, and white. A simple blue and pink garden might combine blue-violet salvia, pink dianthus, and electric blue lobelia.

If warm colors are your pleasure, how about making a sunset-hued garden? Plant daylilies in red, orange, and yellow, and golden rudbeckia or coreopsis; tone them down, if you like, with some white nicotiana, and add a few small yellow marigolds up front. Or how about a combination of pink and red poppies with pink, lavender, and white foxgloves?

Other warm-toned combinations include golden sunflowers and achillea, with red and

A pink and blue bed with the look of a cottage garden, composed entirely of common flowers.

orange dahlias or nasturtiums; or red and orange daylilies with yellow coreopsis and an edging of nasturtiums. Or you might mix a background of black-eyed susans or gloriosa daisies with some African marigolds and a foreground of nasturtiums.

For autumn interest, surround a clump of pennisetum (foxtail grass) or another modest-sized ornamental grass with clumps of Autumn Joy sedum and mums in assorted shades of russet and bronze.

Complementary and contrasting color schemes make the most daring and dramatic color statements. A simple, bright but attractive combination for containers or a small garden bed in a sunny spot uses tall yellow marigolds, purple basil, and small yellow marigolds.

Blue and yellow gardens are contrasting without being jarring, and can be quite lovely. One way to experiment with these colors is to plant a simple tub garden of blue salvia and golden coreopsis. Soft yellow *Coreopsis verticillata* 'Moonbeam' is especially lovely. Or you could create a small bed or border with deep gold achillea, the violet-blue bell-shaped blossoms of campanula or spiky blue salvia, bright yellow coreopsis, and rich blue lobelia.

Adding white to a blue and yellow garden softens and lightens the colors. Consider, for instance, an oval island bed of yellow daylilies, white achillea or classic shasta daisies,

Morning glories create a blooming bower in a single growing season; plant lots of them.

veronica or blue salvia for a vertical accent, and white sweet alyssum planted as an edging. In the more confined space of a tub or pocket garden, you might choose just a few specimens of achillea, small marguerite daisies, and campanula.

The simplest color schemes are monochromatic—shades of a single color. One of the most elegant is an all-white or white-and-silver garden. White gardens have a restrained but refreshing quality about them, and they positively shimmer at dusk, on cloudy days, and in the soft moonlight of a summer night. One simple white combination consists, front to back, of tall cleome or cosmos, snapdragons (choose Rocket or another tall variety), zinnias or nicotiana, and sweet alyssum or white lobelia. A white and silver garden might mix snapdragons, nicotiana, daisies, zinnias, and cosmos with silvery lamb's ears, dusty miller, or artemisia, a green groundcover such as vinca or a white-flowered variety of ajuga or lamium, and sweet alyssum.

Chapter Three

Buying Plants

The great advantage of buying plants from a local nursery over ordering through the mail is that you can see what you're getting. Also, plants sold locally are probably suited to your climate. But just as when you order from mail-order suppliers, it is important to buy from a reliable company. There are all sorts of outlets for flowering plants during the spring and summer. Generally speaking, you will not find the best quality plants in a supermarket or discount store. Although many of these places sell garden plants in spring (the plants can often be found lined up on the pavement outside the store), and the prices are usually very reasonable, the plants are unlikely to be very well cared-for during their time at the store. The staffs are not trained in the care of plants, which are only a seasonal sideline for them. The plants may languish on the pavement, wilting in the hot sun for lack of water, suffering damage during exposure to unusually cold nights, and battered by passing feet. In addition, the plants probably came from a large regional or national wholesaler rather than a more local wholesale nursery, and were shipped a great distance to reach the store. All that time in hot, dark trucks and warehouses would stress even the healthiest plants. Chances are, the plants are already in less than top condition by the time they arrive at the retail outlet.

If you do find a plant sale that is just too good to resist in one of these places, be sure to examine the plants very carefully before you buy them. A bit later in this chapter you will find information on how to choose healthy plants. Poor-quality plants will grow more slowly in your garden, and bloom later and less abundantly than healthy plants; they may even die if they are in bad enough shape when you take them home. However low the price, such plants are no bargain.

You will get the healthiest plants and the best service from a reliable local garden center or nursery. But some garden centers are better than others. Here are some tips on how to pick a good establishment.

The plants on display should be healthy and well cared-for, watered regularly and given protection from cold when necessary. The conditions under which the plants are displayed should resemble the conditions they will need in the garden, with plants preferring some shade kept out of direct sun. Many nurseries place flats of shade-loving plants on benches in a lath house, or underneath benches of sun lovers placed in a sunny location.

Look for a good selection of plants. For greatest versatility, plants should be available in lots of a single color, as well as in mixed-color assortments. Look for plants to be put on display close to the time when it is safe to plant them. If flats of tender bedding annuals go on display in a greenhouse in March or April and it will not be warm enough to plant them outdoors until Memorial Day, the plants will not be in peak condition at planting time.

The staff makes a difference, too. Staff people should be familiar with most of the plants they sell, as well as local growing conditions, and willing to answer questions. Friendly, courteous, knowledgeable salespeople are another indication of a good garden center.

A local company that has been in business for a long time will generally be reliable, although a new business can be fine, too, if it is well run.

Ask where the nursery gets the plants they sell. A retail nursery that propagates some its own stock, and gets the rest from local wholesalers, is a better bet than a firm that sells plants shipped from another state.

Look at the labels in the plant containers; ideally, the botanical name should be given as well as the common name, so plants can all be properly identified. Compare prices, too—they can vary.

If there are several garden centers in your area, visit them all and compare what you find. One will probably seem the best to you—the plants will be of good quality, the prices reasonable, and the selection suited to your needs. Or you may find that one establishment has a particularly good selection of annuals, while another has the best assortment of perennials or herbs.

Another potential source of plants is local florist shops, many of which sell plants during the growing season. You will not find as large a selection of plants at a florist—after all, selling outdoor plants is not their primary business—and there will probably be fewer small plants in flats and cell packs. But you will quite possibly find some uncommon, interesting plants that the owner happens to like. Florists are also a good source of tropical plants to grow outdoors in summer. Judge the quality of florists and their plants by the same criteria you will apply to garden centers and nurseries.

If you really haven't got much money to spend on the garden, there is a way to economize and still get good plants, if you want to grow perennials. That is to wait until late summer to buy and plant them. Most local nurseries, garden centers, and florists put unsold perennials on sale toward the end of summer, to make room for chrysanthemums, asters, and other autumn bloomers. If the plants have been well cared-for all summer, and they look healthy, you can buy them at the end of the season and plant them for bloom the following year. The selection will be limited, and you will have to wait until next season to enjoy the flowers, but you will be able to save a considerable amount of money, as much as half the regular cost.

Another strategy is to put in just a few perennials the first year, and plant the rest of the garden with inexpensive annuals. Add more perennials each year until you have the plants you want.

How to Choose the Best Plants

The first thing to remember when trying to choose among the seemingly endless flats of plants for sale is that the biggest plants are not necessarily the best. In fact, they seldom are, for they may have outgrown their small compartments in a market pack, resulting in stress due to an overcrowded root system that can no longer adequately nourish the plant. Big plants on small root systems also suffer greater shock when you transplant them into the garden—they will cease growing until they recover, and will grow rather slowly after that. If you want to buy a bigger, more mature plant, make sure it is growing in a pot that is large enough to accommodate its root system. Do not buy plants that look topheavy or too big for their containers. Plants that are already in bloom when you buy them may drop some of their blossoms after transplanting. The plant will take time to adjust to conditions in the garden, and to regain enough vigor to produce a new crop of flower buds.

Although small transplants are generally more desirable, it is also wise to avoid buying the very smallest plants. Very young seedlings

A statue, some white impatiens, and stones used as edging create a simple pocket garden at the foot of the stairs. The evergreen shrub serves as a backdrop for the flowers.

A pocket garden in the corner of a partly shaded patio combines red and pink impatiens, caladiums, ferns, and the spiky foliage of variegated lilyturf. A lattice screen provides a backdrop, and a small statue becomes the focal point.

*I*mpatiens are classic flowers for planting around trees, but this gardener added a whimsical touch by planting *in* the tree, setting plants in a soil-filled hollow in the trunk.

*S*mall plants, in this case dianthus and sweet alyssum, replace bricks removed from the corner of a patio to create a charming miniature garden.

*T*his mailbox stands amid a multicolored garden of cheery annuals at the end of the driveway.

*M*orning glories make a leafy screen when grown on a trellis, grow netting, or lattice. Or let them cover an arbor to shade a picnic table or lounge chairs.

*F*ragrant sweet peas threaten to engulf two mailboxes in a cloud of pink and green.

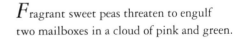

*H*ollyhocks are traditional cottage garden flowers, and they're lovely planted along a fence. These grow and bloom unattended in an old farmyard.

*P*ots, tubs, and windowboxes of petunias, geraniums, and lush ferns dress up an otherwise plain facade. Imagine how much less welcoming the house would look without plants.

*W*indowboxes overflowing with pink petunias bring a touch of country charm to a suburban house. Morning glories have begun a resolute climb up the downspout nearby.

*B*right, hot-colored annuals in containers and small beds create a cheerful, welcoming entrance garden. The cast-iron tub holds red geraniums, and concrete planters are filled with multicolored zinnias. The beds combine spiky scarlet salvia, orange marigolds, impatiens, zinnias, and catharanthus.

*P*ansies and sweet alyssum love cool weather and make a pretty combination in spring gardens and window-boxes.

*T*he big, heart-shaped leaves of caladiums (also known as elephant's ears) bring a shot of color to a shady bed behind a stone wall. The spiky-leaved plants are liriope, or lilyturf, which blooms in early fall.

*B*right marigolds and petunias grow in planters built into the top of a brick wall.

*N*asturtiums add mass to the front of a garden in the ground or containers. The trailing stems tumble all together, creating a sea of warm-colored, funnel-shaped flowers and the distinctive round leaves.

*H*ibiscus is a good plant to add height to a tub garden. With its bold texture and large, exotic-looking blossoms, hibiscus also makes an impressive specimen plant when planted by itself.

*H*ardy chrysanthemums are favorites for fall color. They come in a host of flower forms, from single daisies to full, fluffy pompons, and practically every color except blue.

*T*here is still plenty of color to be found in the garden as summer drifts into fall. Golden rudbeckia and pink physostegia continue to bloom in this late-season garden.

are quite delicate, and more difficult to transplant than plants that are a bit more mature.

The best plants to bring home are stocky, compact, and bushy, with a healthy green color (unless they are a variegated or colored-leaved variety, of course), and leaves spaced close together on a straight, strong stem. The plants should appear vigorous and sturdy. Look for healthy new growth around the top and the tips of branching stems.

Avoid buying plants with tall, lanky, floppy stems with large gaps of bare stem between the leaves. These plants have not been getting enough light, and will probably not perform well in your garden. Plants that have been overfertilized can also look rather elongated, and they tend to put out weak, flaccid leaves on soft stems. Such overstimulated growth is more likely to attract pests than healthy foliage. Pale or yellowish leaf color may indicate insufficient light, lack of nutrients, or overwatering.

Examine the plants carefully for signs of pests and disease. Look especially closely at the tips of the stems, the leaf axils (where leaves join stems), and the undersides of the leaves. If you see small white, greenish, or dark specks, insects are undoubtedly in residence. Aphids may be clustered along stems and in leaf axils. Whiteflies will fly around the plant like a cloud of miniature confetti when the plant is gently shaken. Spider mites leave tell-tale webbing between leaves and stems. Mealybugs look like little globs of cotton stuck in leaf axils and around the growing tips of plants. Don't buy plants infested with insects. The plants themselves will be weakened, and the bugs will in all likelihood spread throughout your garden. If you discover a few bugs after you bring the plants home, either return them to the garden center immediately or quarantine the seedlings and spray them with insecticidal soap according to the package directions. Repeat as necessary until the pests have been eradicated, *then* transplant to the garden.

Check your potential purchases for symptoms of disease and improper care, as well. Look for soft or discolored spots on leaves, discolored veins in leaves, brown, dry leaves or leaf margins (edges). Fuzzy growth on leaves, and soft, darkened areas on leaves or stems are some additional signs of trouble.

Poke a finger into the soil, too. If you can, gently slide a plant partway out of its pot to look at the roots. If you see roots growing out of the drainage hole, or a tight mat of roots immediately inside the drainage hole, the plant is probably rootbound—too big for its pot. Roots growing on the soil surface or, in the case of large plants like trees and shrubs, roots circling the main stem, also indicate a potbound plant. Potbound plants may be stunted in their growth. They will probably recover if you give them special treatment when planting them in your garden (see Chapter Four for information), but they will suffer a setback in their development.

Remember, a poor-quality plant that performs poorly in the garden, or worse, that dies before its time, is no bargain, however inexpensive it was when you bought it.

Choosing Bulbs

When selecting bulbs at the garden center, look for bulbs that are firm and solid. With a few exceptions, such as anemone, bulbs should not be shrivelled or soft. Do not buy bulbs with mold, discolorations, soft spots, or evidence of insect damage. In the case of bulbs that have a basal plate, the flat base from which the roots grow, the basal plate should feel firm when you touch it.

How Big to Buy Them?

Garden centers and nurseries offer plants in a variety of container sizes. Vegetables, herbs, and annuals are available either in compartmentalized market packs, occasionally in undivided flats, and in larger individual pots. Perennials are often sold in four-inch (or one-quart) or six-inch (two-quart) pots, or one- or two-gallon containers, in which they may already be in bloom. How do you know which size to buy? Here are some points to consider.

First, smaller plants are generally easier to handle, and adapt most quickly to the garden environment after transplanting. If you are new to gardening, you may find it difficult to imagine what a small plant will look like when it grows up. The descriptions in Chapter Five can help, and you can also consult other gardening books, and photos in mail-order nursery catalogs for representations of the plants you want in your garden. If you need more than just a few plants—perhaps you need enough sweet alyssum to edge a bed, or enough impatiens to surround a favorite lilac bush—smaller plants in market packs and flats will be the best buy. They will start to grow quickly after transplanting, and come into bloom fairly quickly, as well—perhaps as soon as a week or two. When buying plants in these small containers, choose smaller, but vigorous, specimens. Instead of marigold plants with lots of flowers, choose plants with lots of buds. These plants have channelled their energy into developing strong roots, sturdy stems, and healthy leaves instead of opening flowers, and will reward you with a better display of blooms later on.

If instant color is important to you—you want to plant some containers to decorate the patio for an outdoor party, for instance—buy plants already in bloom in larger containers. Transplant them to the garden after the party. After the first flush of bloom is over it may take the plants some time to settle into their new home and produce more buds, but by then your special occasion will have passed.

If you need a few plants to fill holes in a perennial garden, or you just need enough plants to fill a few pots, the decision may be less obvious. Many garden centers carry perennials in several different size containers, increasing in price with the size of the container. I still prefer to use smaller plants even in these situations, because they are easier to handle during transplanting and make a quicker transition into the garden. But more mature plants in one- or two-gallon containers will also work if you handle them carefully and leave as much of the rootball intact as possible during transplanting (more on this in Chapter Four). The cost of the plants will probably be the most important criterion. Perennial plants that are well along in their growth, perhaps just about to bloom, can cost from six to ten dollars and up per plant. Putting in an entire bed or border of these beauties would run into a sizable sum of money. You will also miss out on the fun of watching little seedlings grow and mature.

How Much to Buy?

Unless you are planting windowboxes or containers in which you know you will only need three of this and six of that, figuring out how many plants to buy will require a certain amount of effort. You can always just guess, and plant the extras in pots or give them to a friend. If you use this seat-of-the-pants method, try to overbuy rather than underbuy, or you may find the nursery sold out of the plant you need by the time you have a chance to go back and buy more.

You might go into a friend or neighbor's garden that is similar in size to your own bed or border, and count how many plants it contains.

This is easy to do early in the season when the plants are young, before they fill their allotted space in the garden. You won't go too far wrong either if you figure that most plants that will remain small can be planted six to twelve inches apart, medium-size plants generally need one to one and one-half feet between them, and big, spreading plants need two feet or more. If you will be massing plants to carpet an area, such as surrounding an established rhododendron or other shrub with impatiens, you will probably need one and one-half to two flats of plants. Spacing distances for individual plants are given in Chapter Five of this book, and on many plant labels; check them before you buy.

If you are planting a half-barrel, probably the most commonly used kind of large container, plan on buying three tall plants, such as geraniums, four to six medium-height plants, and eight to twelve small edging plants for each tub. The container will look a bit sparse when you first plant it, but it will quickly fill in. If you stuff a container with young plants, the larger ones will soon engulf the smaller ones, or all of them may languish for lack of space after a month or so. If you must have an overflowing container, plan to fertilize frequently throughout the season to keep the plants going.

The best way to figure out how many plants you will need in a bed, border, or container is to use a mathematical formula landscape designers use to calculate the approximate number of plants needed to fill a particular area. It takes some time, admittedly, but it is the most reliable method. First, you must figure out the area, in square feet, that the garden, or each type of plant (remember, you will probably be planting in clumps or drifts) will cover. Go out to the garden and measure the area in which you will put the plants.

If the garden or plant area will be square or rectangular, multiply the length of the area by the width. If the area is round, multiply the radius of the circle (the distance from the center to the outer edge) by itself, and then by *pi* (approximately 3.14). To calculate the area of an oval space, measure the radius from the center to one of the near edges of the ellipse, then measure the radius to the far edge of the oval, add them together and divide by 2, to get an average radius. Multiply the average radius by itself and then multiply by *pi* to find the total area.

The next step is to convert the area of the garden from square feet to square inches. To do this, multiply the area in square feet by 144.

Next, look up the plant spacing in Chapter Five, and multiply each plant's spacing distance in inches by itself to find out the total area in square inches to allow for each plant. If the spacing distance is given in feet, convert it to inches before multiplying. (This step is not necessary if you are planting only a single row of plants, such as an edging. In that case all you need to know is the length of the planting area and the distance between plants.) Divide the number of square inches covered by each plant into the total area allotted to that type of plant in the garden to find out roughly how many plants you will need to fill the space.

If you are not sure what kinds of plants you want—perhaps you have several possibilities, depending on what is in stock at the garden center—take a pocket calculator, pad, and pen along with you to the garden center and get the between-plant spacing from the plant labels. Then complete your calculations right there.

If the soil in your garden is of very good quality, you can plant a bit closer than the distance recommended on the plant labels or in Chapter Five. But do not crowd the plants; they need room to grow. I cannot stress enough how important it is to give your plants enough space. A newly planted garden always looks a bit thin until the plants start to grow and fill in. If you plant too close together, the garden will not look so empty when you first plant it, but the plants will never grow as vigorously or bloom as well as they could because they will not have adequate space to develop. Have a little patience—it will pay off.

If the area you will be planting is irregularly shaped, it will be difficult to measure and calculate plant quantities in advance. In such a case you can either use whichever of the formulas given above seems closest to the shape of the garden, or you can just wing it. Buy a couple of market packs or flats of plants, go home and plant them and see how far you get, then go back to the garden center and buy more. The peril of this method is that if the plant you have chosen is a particularly big seller and you cannot get back to buy more for a week or two, the garden center may be sold out before your garden is finished. And if it is the peak of the planting season, you may not want to deal with the crowds at the nursery.

In any case, I think it is best to buy a few more plants than you think you will need, rather than to err on the side of conservatism. That may just be because I love plants. But you can always find room to tuck in a few extra plants somewhere. If your garden is absolutely full, plant the extras in pots to put on your porch or patio.

Making Substitutions

If the garden center doesn't have a particular plant you want, you will have to substitute or go elsewhere. If you are a careful planner, you made a list of second and third choices when you planned the garden. If, like me, you are somewhat less disciplined, you will have to choose an alternate on the spot. Here are some things to think about when choosing a substitute plant.

First, could you use the same plant in a different color? If not, check plant labels to find another plant of similar color, height, and shape. For instance, if you want a yellow daisy-like flower and had chosen a coreopsis that is not in stock, you might be able to substitute heliopsis or rudbeckia. If you were hoping for the spiky blue flowers of veronica, you might be able to substitute a blue salvia, or perhaps physostegia (false dragonhead), which comes in a light lavender-blue.

Plant Substitution Guide

If the garden center doesn't have a plant that you want, here are some questions to ask yourself to find a substitute. Look for plants with qualities similar to those of your original choice.

✪ Does the garden center have the plant in a different color that would also work in your garden?

✪ What is the form of the flower you wanted?
  • spiky and vertical
  • round, ball-shaped
  • daisylike, disc-shaped
  • delicate and fluffy
  • bell-shaped
  • trumpet-shaped

✪ What is the size, form, and texture of the plant?
  • tall, medium, or small

- bold-leaved and sculptural, spiky-leaved and vertical, branched and bushy, sprawling and spreading, low and mounded, climbing or trailing
- ✪ What color are the flowers and when do they bloom?
- ✪ What are the plant's environmental needs (sun, soil, moisture)?

A good plant label will give you lots of information about a plant. In addition to the botanical and common names, you should find the plant's mature height, light needs, spacing distance, and color. The label may also list special qualities like drought tolerance, and there may be a tiny photo of the plant as well.

The garden center staff can be helpful, too. Ask a salesperson about a plant with which you are unfamiliar. Is it bushy or spiky? Will it spread? Are the pink flowers a bright or pale shade, a warm or cool pink?

You could also take this book along with you to the garden center, and read over the Plant Substitution Guide. Then refer to the lists of flowers by color, use in the garden, and other qualities, that appear in the Appendix, to help you find substitute plants.

If you are unfamiliar with the true color of a flower, you will just have to experiment; plant labels and photographs in books and catalogs can be deceiving. One year I planted a dwarf snapdragon described as lilac-pink, and it turned out to be a bright rose color that was almost red-violet to my eye. But surprises are part of the fun of gardening, and there's always next year.

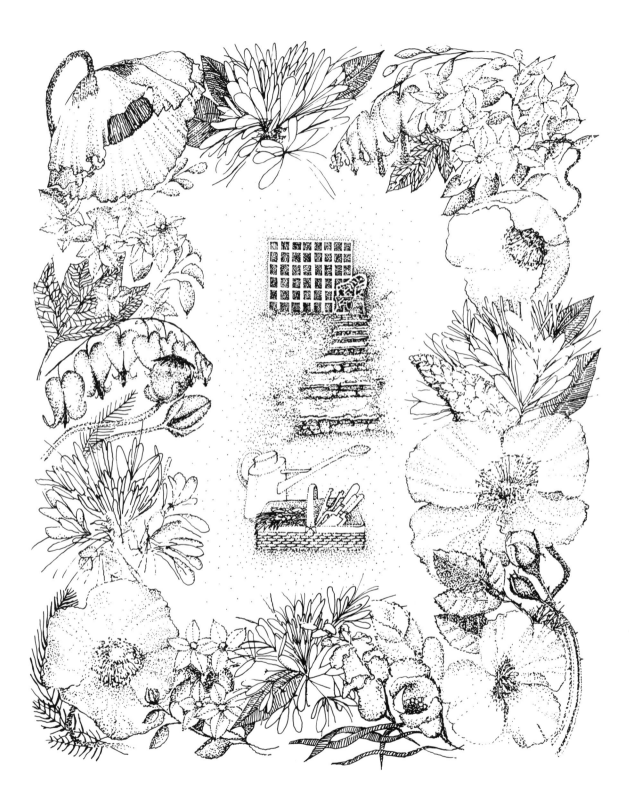

Chapter Four

Planting and Caring for the Garden

It is a good idea to prepare the garden soil for planting before you buy any plants. In an existing garden, soil preparation can be done as soon as the ground thaws and the excess water from the melting ice drains off in spring. An old-fashioned farmer's trick is still the best way to tell when the soil is ready to work. Scoop up a handful of soil and squeeze it into a ball, then open your fingers. If the ball of soil stays tightly packed together, the soil is still too wet to work. But if the ball slowly crumbles, the soil is dry enough for digging.

It is important not to dig the soil too early in spring. Working wet soil can cause it to compact, closing up the air spaces between the individual particles of soil. Compacted soil provides a poor growing medium for plants. It becomes dense and heavy, making it difficult for essential air and water to penetrate to plant roots. When the ground does become wet, the water drains off very slowly, and the garden becomes waterlogged. Plant roots, which grow in the spaces between soil particles, have a difficult time; they may be unable to develop large enough and quickly enough to support vigorous, healthy topgrowth. For the sake of your plants, do not be in too much of a rush to get into the garden in spring.

Sandy soils are light, porous, and quick to drain, and will be ready for planting earlier in spring than denser clay soils.

If your garden is already established, all you need to do in spring is turn over the soil with a spade or tiller and work in a one-inch layer of compost, leaf mold, or other organic matter. It is important to add organic matter to the soil every year. Soil rich in organic matter provides a good growing medium for plants. It retains moisture while still draining well, and is rich in beneficial microorganisms that assist in the breakdown of minerals and other nutrient sources into forms plants can use.

If you garden organically, you should also work in some animal manure to provide nitrogen, a season ahead of planting if it is fresh; till it into the soil in fall. Composted animal manures can be added closer to planting if you wish. Phosphorus and potassium, the other two major nutrients necessary for plant growth, can be supplied organically with rock powders such as rock or colloidal phosphate and granite dust, or from one of the other sources listed in the table, Organic Fertilizers. Rock powders are best added to the soil the autumn before planting, because they break down very slowly and it takes time for their nutrients to become available to plants. Most organic materials break down slowly but some, notably wood ashes (which supply potassium), blood meal (nitrogen), and fish meal (nitrogen, phosphorus, and potassium) break down more quickly and can be worked into the soil when you cultivate in spring.

If you opt for one of the packaged, pre-blended organic fertilizers now on the market, follow the package directions regarding its use. If you get into a regular routine of adding organic fertilizers in spring before planting, and in fall when you clean up the garden for winter, there will always be plenty of nutrients available for your plants. Organic fertilizers are mild, for the most part, so there is little danger of overfeeding the garden. To be sure the fertilizer you choose is really organic and not just using the term as a marketing ploy, read the label carefully. It should list ingredients like the organic materials in the table, Organic Fertilizers.

If you prefer to use nonorganic fertilizers, such as an all-purpose 5-10-5 formula, you will not fertilize until you are ready to actually put the plants in the ground. Again, follow the package directions regarding application. Never use more fertilizer than the package directions indicate. These plant foods are very concentrated; using too much can burn delicate roots, and the excess that cannot be taken up by roots is carried away by groundwater and may end up in the water table. Fertilizer runoff is a major source of water pollution in the United States, especially in agricultural areas, and environmentally aware gardeners do not want to contribute to the problem.

Organic Fertilizers

The following organic materials add nutrients, as well as organic matter, to garden soil. Apply them individually, or look for them in pre-blended natural fertilizers. Use packaged materials according to package directions.

All plants need a combination of nutrients in order to grow well, but keep in mind that foliage plants need a higher proportion of nitrogen to promote lush leaf growth, and flowering plants need lots of phosphorus to perform their best.

Nitrogen Sources

Animal manures (cow, horse, chicken, sheep)
Blood meal or dried blood
Bone meal (small amount of nitrogen)
Coffee grounds
Cottonseed meal (for acid-loving plants)
Fish emulsion, fish products
Guano
Legume cover crops (alfalfa, beans, clover tilled into soil at end of season)
Soybean meal

Phosphorus Sources

Bone meal
Colloidal phosphate
Blood meal or dried blood (small amount)
Fish emulsion, fish products (small amount)
Guano
Mushroom compost (from commercial mushroom farms)
Phosphate rock

Potassium Sources

Fish emulsion, fish products (small amount)
Granite dust
Greensand
Seaweed
Wood ashes

Sources of Trace Elements

Kelp, seaweed
Chelated minerals
Epsom salts (magnesium)
Borax (boron)

When you dig the garden, you can leave the soil surface rough until you are ready to plant. Then rake it smooth to level the surface and create a fine-textured planting area that is free of large stones and clods of earth.

If you are starting a new garden or rejuvenating a long-neglected garden, you have more work ahead of you. You must first clear away all the weeds and plant debris or, if you are carving a new garden out of a lawn, you have to remove the sod. Taking up sod is hard work, but here is how to do it. First, mark out the garden area with stakes and string. Drive a spade more or less horizontally under the layer of grass, and push upward on the handle to pull the sod away from the soil. Or you can dig the sod into the soil and wait for it to decompose. You will have to do this in fall if you want to plant the following spring, and clumps will remain in the soil even then.

If you pile the chunks of sod you remove from the garden site in an out-of-the-way place, in a year or so it will decompose and you can return it to the garden. Stack the turves in alternating layers, with like sides together, grass to grass, then root to root.

Of course, the lawn will attempt to creep back into the garden area from all sides. Installing edging strips around the perimeter will help prevent the grass from encroaching.

To dig the soil in a new garden, remove soil to a depth of about a foot. Start at one end of the bed and work your way across in rows. After digging the first row, pile the soil removed from it in a wheelbarrow. Examine the soil now exposed in the garden. If it appears dense, drive a garden fork into it and wiggle it back and forth to loosen the soil. Dig the next row of soil and pile it into the trench left when you dug the first row. Break up any clods and remove as many stones as you can. Then loosen the subsoil in row two. Work your way across the garden, and finally, dump the soil from the wheelbarrow into the last trench.

Gardening can be very good exercise, but doing the hard work now will make gardening easier in the future.

If your garden is sizable, rent a tiller to turn the soil after you remove the sod.

When the soil has been dug, work in whatever fertilizers and soil conditioners you wish to add.

In subsequent years, digging will be lots easier, unless your soil is heavy clay. In that case it will take several years of painstaking digging and adding organic matter to create an easily workable soil. In lighter soils, all you will probably need to do is add organic matter and then loosen the soil with a garden fork before planting.

If You Can't Plant Right Away

Try to buy plants when you are ready to put them into the garden. Plants in market packs are especially vulnerable, because the soil in the small compartments dries out very quickly, with little to buffer the plants from moisture and temperature fluctuations. If you must hold the plants for any reason—an unexpected rainstorm, for instance, or unannounced visitors showing up at your door—there are a few things you can do to hold the plants in reasonably good condition until you can plant them.

Set the containers of plants in a sheltered, shady spot, out of direct sun and protected from wind. Check them frequently to make sure they are not drying out. Plants in market packs will need watering at least once a day in warm or windy weather. Given this kind of care, your plants should survive in good shape for a week or two. Plants in larger containers may be held even longer if they are not severely potbound. But eventually, all nursery plants will outgrow their containers. The best way to ensure strong, continuous growth is to get them into the ground as soon as you can.

If you are a weekend gardener with a country house, it is imperative that you buy only as many plants as you will be able to transplant in a weekend. Plants in market packs and flats will not survive for a week without water. If you simply cannot get all your plants into the ground, leave them with a friend who can water them during the week.

Hardening-Off Plants

If the plants you buy have been kept in a greenhouse or moved indoors at night at the garden center, you will have to harden them off before planting them, just as you would transplants you started indoors from seed. Hardening-off gradually accustoms the plants to the kinds of conditions they will face outdoors in the garden. If you do not harden-off your plants, they will suffer a greater degree of transplant shock, and may be damaged or even killed by exposure to colder, windier, wetter, or drier conditions than they are used to.

To harden-off plants, place them outdoors each day in a sheltered spot, perhaps under a tree or against the wall of the house beneath an overhanging roof. Start by putting the plants outside for a few hours the first day, and leave them out for a longer time each day thereafter, moving them back indoors, or to an unheated sunporch, at night. After a week of gradually lengthening exposure, leave the plants outdoors overnight. The next day you can plant them in the garden.

If you cannot accommodate this schedule because you are away at work all day or only use the house on weekends, be sure to purchase plants that have already been hardened-off at the nursery. Ask before you buy them.

When to Plant

Plants that are described as hardy or half-hardy can tolerate varying degrees of cold. Hardy plants can survive the coldest (and hottest) average temperatures in a given location without any special protection. Trees and shrubs survive year after year in regions where they are hardy. Hardy perennials die back to the ground in fall, but their roots live through winter in a dormant state.

Hardy annual plants by definition cannot live beyond a single growing season, but their seeds can. Annuals that self-sow and produce new seedlings the next spring, such as sweet alyssum, are considered hardy. Half-hardy plants can usually withstand an occasional light frost, but will be damaged or killed by prolonged exposure to subfreezing temperatures.

Both hardy and half-hardy plants can be put into the garden in spring, while there is still a chance of an occasional light frost.

Tender plants cannot tolerate any frost whatsoever, and need warm soil in order to grow well. Do not plant them until later in spring, when you are sure there will be no more frosty nights in your garden. Consult the USDA Plant Hardiness Zone Map or call your local USDA County Extension Service office to find out the average date of the last spring frost in your area. You can find the zone map in most gardening encyclopedias, although books published before 1991 will not have the revised version of the map. Wait a week or two beyond the last frost date to plant tender plants. Better yet, if you have a lilac bush or an oak tree, wait until their leaves are an inch or two long. Both lilacs and oak trees begin to put out their leaves around the time of the last frost. They provide a better guide to safe planting times for tender plants than do frost dates, which are only an average and fluctuate from year to year.

The best day for planting is one that is overcast and calm, with moderate temperatures. If the temperature is quite warm, plant in the morning or late afternoon, rather than in the midday heat. If the weather turns unexpectedly cold or rainy, wait until it settles before you set out plants.

How to Plant

Water the plants several hours before you plan to transplant them. Take a bucket of tepid (neither hot nor cold) water along with you to the garden. If the plants are growing in an undivided flat, you must also "block" the plants to separate their root systems before planting. Do not just pull the plants apart; that would cause damage to the roots. To block plants, cut down into the soil with a sharp knife, lengthwise and crosswise, as if you were cutting a pan of brownies. You will have each seedling in the center of its own little block of soil. Ideally, blocking should be done several days before transplanting, but you can do it right when you transplant, if necessary.

Dig the planting holes before you remove any of the plants from their pots. You want to transfer the plants from the pots directly into the ground so their delicate roots will not have a chance to dry out (which would shut down growth). Dig the holes at the correct spacing distance for each plant. Spacing distances are given in Chapter Five of this book, and may also be found on many of the nursery labels in the pots. Although the holes may look too far apart when you first put in the small plants, avoid the temptation to plant any closer

together. You must allow the plants sufficient room to grow and develop or they will look anemic all season. Crowded plants are also more likely to experience pest and disease problems. You can fudge a bit in containers that you will fertilize regularly throughout the growing season, or if your soil is exceptionally fertile. Otherwise, follow the recommended spacings. Your patience will be rewarded with vigorous, healthy plants as the season progresses.

Make the planting holes large enough to hold each plant's rootball, and deep enough so the plant sits at about the same level it was growing in its container.

To remove a plant from an individual pot, tap the bottom with the handle of a trowel to loosen the plant. Turn over the pot and support the top of the soilball with one hand, placing a finger on either side of the stem for support. With the other hand, slide the pot off the rootball. If the plant does not slide easily from the pot, set it back down. Insert an old kitchen knife vertically into the pot, between the inner wall and the soil; run the knife around the inside of the pot to loosen the soilball. Turn the plant over, supporting under the rootball with your hand or a trowel. Try to leave as much of the soilball intact as possible. Set the plant carefully in the planting hole and fill in with soil around the roots. Water to settle the soil around the plant and insure good root contact, then fill in any holes that remain.

If the plant is rootbound, before planting try to tease out some of the larger roots from the rootball, and gently separate the roots without breaking them. If the plant is *severely* rootbound, with a mass of roots so tightly packed together that you cannot pull them apart without breaking them, take a sharp knife and make three vertical cuts about halfway up into the root mass, starting from the bottom. Carefully spread apart the rootball along these cuts before putting the plant into the planting hole.

To remove a plant from a market pack, tap or press lightly on the bottom of the cell, to loosen the plant. If the plant does not slide easily out of the cell, cut the plastic with scissors and tear it away from the soilball. Grasp the plant *very gently* by two upper leaves (but not the growing tip), and slip it out of the cell. It is best to hold the plant by the leaves rather than the stem or the growing tip at the very top of the stem. Damage to a couple of leaves will not harm the plant, but damage to the stem or growing tip could kill it. When the plant is out of the cell, support it underneath and plant as described above.

Planting in Containers

One of the best things about gardening in pots, tubs, hanging baskets, and windowboxes is that you can give plants an ideal soil mix. There is also far less hard physical labor involved in container gardening—you don't have to dig the garden each spring, for one thing. The drawback is that potted plants are almost totally dependent on you, the gardener, for the water and nutrients they need in order to grow; you will have to water and fertilize frequently.

Planting in containers starts with blending the potting mix. The best growing medium for plants in pots or other containers is loose and porous in texture, well-aerated, and allows excess water to drain off quickly while still retaining enough moisture for plant roots. Potting mixes are lighter-textured than most garden soils.

The relationship between plants and soil is complex, but a basic understanding of it will help you to better comprehend what plants need to grow strong and vigorous. We say that plants grow *in* the ground, but actually, the roots grow in the spaces between individual particles of soil. Air and water also travel through these spaces. Water is the medium that carries the nutrients plants need to fuel their growth, and air is important to the survival of soil microorganisms that assist in the transfer of moisture and nutrients from soil to roots.

When soil is watered, from rain or by the gardener, the water moves through the spaces between soil particles, driving out the air. If excess water cannot drain away, fresh air cannot enter, and eventually roots will suffocate. The root rot that inevitably occurs when soil remains waterlogged is caused more by the presence of too little air than by the presence of too much water. In dense, heavy soil, the particles are so close together that there is little room for air, water, and roots. In the confined space of a container, the problem of standing water is magnified because roots have nowhere else to go; they cannot grow around or below the soggy area. That is why a light soil mix is so important for plants in pots.

A good potting mix should contain a lightening agent for porosity (usually vermiculite, perlite, or sharp builder's sand), organic matter (leaf mold, compost, or peat moss), and additional nutrients from fertilizers of either natural or manmade origin. The mix may or may not contain soil, as well. I personally believe some soil is helpful in potting media to give them body; I find soilless mixes too light for plants growing outdoors. But you will have to make your own decision. Just bear in mind that unless you purchase a preblended potting mix with fertilizer added, soilless mixes contain no nutrients for plants, and you will have to add fertilizer when you mix the ingredients, or use a liquid fertilizer regularly when you water the plants. Also be aware that many of the commercial products labeled as "potting soil" are too dense to use by themselves, no matter what the package says. If you open a bag of potting mix and find it to be mostly soil, even if the soil is dark-colored and humusy, I recommend mixing the soil with an equal volume of peat, perlite, or vermiculite before using it as a potting medium.

One other material you can consider adding to potting media is a water-retentive polymer. A number of these polymer products are now on the market, to be added to potting mixes and garden soils to increase their ability to hold moisture, and cut down on watering frequency. Gardeners report varying results with these products. They are generally effective, but some people don't like the texture, and others find that adding too much of the polymer to the soil (which is easy to do, since they absorb surprising amounts of water) causes the soil to overflow from the pot when the plants are watered. If you have a lot of potted plants outdoors and have difficulty keeping them moist, a polymer is probably worth a try. Just be prepared to experiment until you find exactly the right amount to use.

Here are a few recipes for making your own potting mixes. For ease of reference later on, the formulas are summarized in the box, Recipes for Potting Mixes. A very simple formula is to blend two parts of a commercial soilless growing mix, such as Pro-Mix, with one part of potting soil or garden loam. Or mix one part soil, one part sharp builder's sand, and one part peat moss, with a tablespoon of bone meal added for each quart of the mixture. Another all-purpose medium combines two parts soil with one part

crumbled compost, one part sand, perlite, or vermiculite, and a tablespoon of bone meal added per quart. For plants that need a rich, fertile medium, mix one part soil, two parts crumbled compost, and one part perlite or vermiculite. If you prefer a soilless mix, you can concoct one from three parts peat moss and one part sand, perlite, or vermiculite. Unless you are growing acid-loving plants, add three-fourths cup of ground limestone to each bushel of the mixture to neutralize the acidity of the peat.

Recipes for Potting Mixtures

All-Purpose Mix #1

2 parts commercial growing mix
1 part potting soil or garden loam

All-Purpose Mix #2

1 part potting soil or garden loam
1 part sharp builder's sand, vermiculite, or perlite
1 part peat moss
1 tablespoon bone meal per quart of mix (optional)

All-Purpose Mix #3

2 parts potting soil or garden loam
1 part crumbled compost
1 part sharp sand, perlite, or vermiculite
1 tablespoon bone meal per quart (optional)

Rich Mix

1 part potting soil or garden loam
2 parts crumbled compost
1 part perlite or vermiculite

Planting and Caring for the Garden / 77

Soilless Potting Mix

3 parts peat moss

1 part vermiculite, perlite, or sharp sand

3/4 cup ground limestone per bushel of mix (except for acid-loving plants)

When planting in containers, some gardeners like to put a layer of gravel or filter charcoal (not barbecue briquettes, which contain chemicals that are harmful to plants) in the bottom of each pot to promote drainage, even in pots with drainage holes. Others say it is unnecessary. I have grown potted plants both ways and have never really noticed a difference in their performance either way. One thing gravel will do is keep soil from leaking out the drainage hole in the bottom of the pot. But you can purchase a plastic mesh material to do the same thing, if you are so inclined, and I have found that a small piece of paper towel placed over the drainage hole, inside the pot, also works just fine. It allows runoff water to drain out but keeps the soil from escaping with it.

To plant containers, fill them to within a half inch of the top with potting mix and water well to settle the mix. Add more mix and water again. When the mix is moist, and fills the pots to within one-half to one inch of the rim, the container is ready for planting. Do not fill pots all the way to the top or you will not have any space left for watering. If you are using a peat-based potting mix, moisten it before putting it in the containers. Peat sheds water when it is dry, and you will have to stir or knead the mix to moisten it. This is lots easier to do when the mix is in a pile on the ground, or in a wheelbarrow, or still in the bag, than when it is in a bunch of different containers.

When the containers are ready, dig planting holes with a trowel and plant the same way you would transplant into the garden. Water to settle the soil around the plants, and fill in any holes that remain.

If you are putting several kinds of plants in a large tub or planter box, plant the plants that will grow tallest first, and put them in the center of the box. Then work outward, planting the smallest plants around the outer edges of the box last. In the case of a container that will be viewed only from one side, like a windowbox, put the tallest plants in the back and work out toward the front.

Caring for New Transplants

To help new transplants adjust to their new home in the garden, give them some special care during their first week outdoors. Water when necessary to keep the soil evenly moist—but not soggy—while the plants begin to send new roots out into the garden soil. If the transplants are young plants, and they have been moved from a partly shaded spot at the nursery to a location in full sun in your garden, you may want to cover them lightly with shade netting for their first few days in the garden. If the weather turns extremely windy or a severe thunderstorm comes your way, it is a good idea to stake the new plants or cover them with baskets or boxes weighted down with stones until the winds die down. Otherwise the plants may topple over because they have not yet had a chance to send roots deeply enough into the soil to provide a strong anchor for the topgrowth.

Planting Bulbs

Hardy bulbs that grace our gardens with their bright blossoms in spring—daffodils and narcissus, tulips, hyacinths, crocus and the like—are planted in autumn. Plant them at least a month before the ground is likely to freeze, so they have time to develop roots. Tender,

To plant the mixed tub garden shown here, you would first put in the central coreopsis, then plant the marigolds around them, and finally, the edging of sanvitalia.

summer-blooming bulbs such as gladiolus and dahlia are planted in spring after all danger of frost is past.

You can dig the planting holes with a trowel, or a bulb planting tool that removes a plug of soil when you push it into the soil and pull it back out. If you are planting an entire bed of bulbs, you may find it simpler to excavate the soil in the whole bed to the necessary depth, lay out the bulbs, and then replace the soil.

To create the most effective display, plant bulbs in groups, rather than dotting them about the garden individually. Plant groups of three in a triangular arrangement, larger groups in a curved drift. If you want a naturalistic, random look from a lot of bulbs, you can toss the bulbs in handfuls over the ground, and plant them where they land.

Planting depth varies with the size of the bulb, but a general guideline is to make the planting depth one and one-half times the diameter of the bulb. Put a handful of bonemeal or bulb fertilizer in the bottom of each planting hole and mix it into the soil before setting the bulb in the hole.

Caring for the Garden as It Grows

The single most important piece of advice I could give anyone about caring for a garden is to keep up with it and not neglect it. An hour or two a week in your garden, or half an hour several days a week, is really all you need to keep the garden looking good, unless your garden is quite extensive or you are growing plants that need special care. If you keep up with the basic maintenance of the garden, the work will never become overwhelming. Small weeds are easier to pull than big ones. A few pests are easier to eliminate than a full-blown infestation. Spending time in your garden on a regular basis will enable you to spot and deal with problems before they get out of hand.

Ignore this advice at your own peril; weeds left unpulled in June will overrun the garden in July. And there is no sorrier sight than an overgrown, unkempt, weed-choked garden that started out with such promise at the beginning of the season.

Following is a rundown of essential garden chores.

Watering

All plants need water to grow, although the amount and frequency of moisture needed varies from plant to plant. Unless you grow drought-tolerant plants, or live in a moist climate, you will undoubtedly have to water your garden at least occasionally to supplement rainfall. With the threat of more serious and widespread water shortages looming over us all, it is essential for gardeners to use water as efficiently as possible to avoid wasting this precious resource.

There are several ways to conserve water and still give your plants the moisture they need to grow well. First, water only when it is necessary. The old rule of giving the garden an inch of water a week does not hold true for all plants in all soils and climates. A garden in heavy clay soil in a cool, cloudy location will need less watering; a seashore garden in sandy soil and hot sun will need more than an inch of water a week. Instead of blindly following rules, or setting the timer on an automatic watering system and leaving it the same all summer, water your plants when they need it.

The best way to tell when the garden needs water is to poke a finger into the soil. When the ground feels dry more than an inch or two below the surface, it is time to water. Do not wait to water until your plants wilt or appear limp; wilting indicates severe water stress. Some plants look a bit flaccid in mid-afternoon on a hot, sunny day, but will perk up again later on, toward dusk. That does not necessarily mean they are suffering water stress. But if plants look wilted in the morning or evening they are in trouble. Give them water immediately. Your goal should be to get water to plants before they become stressed, and checking the soil regularly as described above will let you do so. Plants that have been stressed will grow more slowly and bloom later and less profusely than healthier specimens.

When it is time to water the plants, water deeply so the moisture soaks far down into the soil. Deep watering encourages plants to send roots downward into the soil, where they will be able to find more water during dry weather. You will save water, because you will have to water less often. The plants will be less dependent on you to supply all the moisture they need. On the other hand, if you water lightly and often—say, a quick sprinkling from the hose every day—the plants will concentrate their roots near the soil surface, where they will be vulnerable to dry weather and hot sun. A second way to conserve water, then, is to water deeply and less often.

A third way to reduce watering is to mulch the garden. Mulching slows the evaporation of moisture from the soil. Mulches are discussed later in this chapter.

Six Ways to Save Water

1. Water plants only when they need it.
2. When you do water, water deeply and thoroughly, but stop immediately if water starts to run off.
3. Mulch the garden.
4. Water at the base of plants, rather than from overhead.
5. Collect and recycle water from dehumidifiers, air conditioners, and rain gutters. In drought areas, learn how to safely recycle for the garden "graywater" from laundry, dishwashing, and other household uses.
6. Grow drought-tolerant plants.

To use the least amount of water, it is important to get the water to the plants in the most efficient possible way. It is best to apply water directly to the soil, where roots can use it. Soaker hoses and drip irrigation systems are two ways to water at ground level. Both are preferable to the traditional method of watering from above with a hose or automatic sprinkler. Overhead watering wastes a lot of water, because the water must filter down through the leaves to get to the soil, and much is lost to evaporation, especially on a hot day, before it can reach the ground. Another drawback to overhead watering, if plants are watered late in the day, is the possibility of mildew and fungus developing when foliage remains wet at night. Watering from above does offer the advantages of cleansing foliage

and helping to cool plants in hot weather. If you must water with a hand-held hose, do it in the morning or late afternoon, avoiding the hottest part of the day when evaporation would be greatest. If you water late in the afternoon, be sure there are a few hours of daylight left so plant leaves will be dry by dark. You could also get a bubbler attachment for your hose and lay the hose on the ground in the garden, moving it around to water all the plants.

The best approach, though, is to install a drip irrigation system or soaker hoses in the garden. Soaker hoses are made of canvas or fiber, and allow water to trickle slowly through pores in their walls. The hoses connect to one another and to an outdoor faucet that you need turn on only partway. Lay the hoses through the garden early in the season when the plants are still small. If their appearance bothers you, cover them with mulch.

You can put together a drip irrigation system from a kit, or buy the components individually. Drip systems use lengths of narrow plastic tubing with small perforations along the sides. The tubing is connected with couplings and can be hooked up to a timer for automatic operation. Drip irrigation systems are installed under the soil surface. There are systems for container gardens as well as in-ground gardens. The equipment is rather costly, and requires a fair amount of labor to install, but once in place drip irrigation is effective and convenient, and does not detract from the garden's appearance.

Watering Plants in Containers

Because the volume of soil in a container—even a large tub —is so much smaller than that in even a minuscule garden in the ground, it dries out rapidly outdoors. Plants growing in containers need to be watered much more frequently than plants growing in the ground. In hot weather, especially on windy days, you will need to water potted plants in all but large tubs and barrels daily, small pots perhaps twice a day, to give the plants the moisture they need. The smaller the container, the faster it will dry out. Plastic pots do not allow moisture to evaporate as quickly as porous clay pots, and grouping potted plants together also helps. You might also wish to add a water-retentive polymer to your potting mix, as described earlier. These products are now widely available in garden centers. But you will still need to water container plants often in summer. Check them every day—or twice a day—and water whenever the soil feels dry below the surface.

If you are watering plants in pots set inside decorative cachepots that do not have drainage holes, it is important to remove the excess water that is not taken up by plant roots. Letting plants sit in water for extended periods leads to root rot and, eventually, their demise. Check the pots approximately fifteen minutes after watering. If any water remains in the bottom of the cachepot, lift out the inner pot and pour off the water.

Add a water-soluble fertilizer to the water once a month when you water annuals growing in containers. Regular fertilizing is especially important if the plants are growing in a soilless potting mix. Follow the package directions when adding fertilizer to the water.

If, despite your best efforts, a small to medium-size plant in an individual pot becomes limp and starts to wilt, you can probably save it if the water stress is not too severe and you act quickly. Here's what to do. Fill with water a bucket that is large enough to comfortably hold the pot; it must be deeper than the pot is tall. Grasp the pot by its upper rim with both hands, and lower it into the water until the pot is completely submerged. The plant will probably not be totally immersed. You will hear a bubbling sound as air is forced from the dry potting mix and replaced by water. When the bubbling stops, the soil is thoroughly saturated. Remove the pot from the bucket and let the excess water drain off. Mist the foliage with lukewarm water and set the pot in a shady place. Unless the plant was badly damaged by drought, it should recover over the next few hours.

This method is the quickest way to completely moisten dry soil, but it is only really feasible for plants of modest size. If a plant or plants in a large, heavy container that is too heavy to lift become wilted, you will have to rehydrate the soil with traditional watering methods—using a hose or watering can. Just be sure to water the dry soil thoroughly. Watch for water to begin leaking from the drainage holes in the bottom of the pot; when it does you can be reasonably sure the soil is saturated.

Weeding and Mulching

There are numerous arguments to be made in favor of mulching the garden, which are discussed below, but mulches are not for everyone. If you choose not to mulch your garden, you will have to weed it. Not only does a weedy garden look messy, weeds are tough, opportunistic plants that will take over if given half a chance. They will outcompete less aggressive garden plants for water and nutrients, and eventually the weeds will overwhelm the garden.

The best way to keep weeds at bay is simply to pull them regularly. Make it a point to weed the garden once a week, or to pull a few weeds every day. Weeding is really not such an odious chore, especially if you keep up with it. It can actually be rather soothing—the sort of simple physical activity in a tranquil setting that can provide an antidote to a hectic, stressful day. Think of weeding as an opportunity to spend time in your garden and appreciate your plants (after all, isn't that why you grow them?). Feel the warm sun on your back, or the cool breeze in your hair. Listen to the songs of birds and the hum of insects. Watch bees and butterflies go about their business.

There are also some ways to make weeding easier and less time-consuming. Weeds are easiest to pull when they are small, and when the soil is moist and loose. But don't weed immediately after a rain, when the soil is still quite wet, or you may cause the soil to compact when you step on it. Also, working around wet plants can spread disease organisms among them. Let the plants dry off, and let the soil dry partially, too, before you weed. You can use a hoe or cultivator to loosen the soil, if you wish, then pull out the weeds. Simply hoeing the garden will chop off the tops of the weeds but leave the roots in the ground, a situation that is not desirable from my point of view. Regular cultivation, when done thoroughly, loosens and aerates the soil, in addition to loosening weeds, which is beneficial.

When you pull weeds, try to pull out the roots, not just break off the tops. Roots left in the soil will grow a whole new crop of weeds in short order.

If you cannot keep up with the weeding as well as you should, at least try to get the weeds out of the garden before they go to seed. If they drop their seeds, you will have an even bigger weed problem. Another tip: do not put weeds that are going to seed on the compost pile. If you do, you will spread the seeds through the garden with the compost and have a nice crop to deal with next year! Weeds that have not gone to seed are fine for the compost heap.

For the sake of comfort, I strongly recommend buying a foam rubber kneeling pad, or a set of knee pads, to use when weeding. Or you might want to get a kneeling bench that you can flip over and sit on as well.

If communing with nature on your knees is not your idea of a good time, you can virtually eliminate the need to weed by mulching the garden.

Mulching, quite simply, involves covering the soil surface between and around plants with any of a number of organic or inorganic materials. Depending on the material used, a mulch can warm the soil in early spring, so plants and seeds can go into the ground as early as possible, it can help conserve moisture and keep down weeds in summer, delay the freezing of the soil in fall to permit later harvests of root vegetables, or keep the ground frozen in winter to prevent alternate freezing and thawing that can damage the roots of perennials.

Organic mulches are the most versatile and attractive in the garden. They also add organic matter to the soil as they decompose. Organic materials to use for mulch include wood chips, bark chips, cocoa bean hulls, straw, salt marsh hay, shredded leaves, and sawdust. See the table, A Guide to Mulches, for information on the benefits and drawbacks of these and other materials.

The best time to lay down a summer mulch is after the soil has thoroughly warmed in spring, and plants are several inches high. If you put down the mulch too early, it will actually keep the soil colder longer, and delay the planting of tender plants. A one- to two-inch layer of fine-textured material is usually sufficient; coarser materials require more depth in order to provide good coverage. The mulch blocks light from reaching the soil between garden plants, and thus prevents most weed seeds from germinating. Mulch also keeps the soil surface loose and crumbly, because the sun cannot bake it into a hard crust. Thus, any weeds that do grow can be pulled out easily. All in all, a summer mulch is a tremendous work saver.

The other important time to mulch an ornamental garden, at least if the garden includes perennials, is in winter. Alternate freezing and thawing of soil in winter can cause the ground to heave and buckle. This action can push the roots of perennials right out of the soil, exposing them to the harsh weather, which can kill them. The idea behind mulching in winter is to keep the soil cold so it stays frozen during winter thaws. Do not lay winter mulch until after the ground has frozen solid. In early spring, when the sun can begin to thaw the soil, pull the mulch aside to let the soil warm.

Commercial growers of strawberries and vegetables sometimes like to mulch early crops with black plastic to speed growth in early spring. Home gardeners can do this, too. Plastic mulches will also keep down weeds and hold soil moisture. The usual technique is to lay the mulch, burying the edges to hold the plastic in place, then cut X-shaped slits or holes in the plastic through which to insert the plants. Allow enough space around the stem for the stem to reach its mature size without completely filling the hole in the plastic, so that water can get to plant roots. A black plastic mulch is pretty unattractive in a flower or herb garden, so you may want to cover it with soil. Also, the plastic may hold too much heat in the soil at the expense of your plants, especially if the plastic is exposed to the sun.

A Guide to Mulches

Bark chips	Available in several sizes. Brown, turn gray as they age. Lay down a 2-inch layer of large chips, 1 to 2 inches of smaller chips. Add nitrogen fertilizer to soil at end of season, as chips start to decompose.
Cocoa bean hulls	Expensive but very attractive, and they smell like chocolate. Spread 2 inches deep.
Compost	Use 2 to 4 inches deep. At end of season till it right into the soil.
Grass clippings	Lay down a 1- to 2-inch layer, and allow clippings to dry out before applying, or mix them with another material to prevent them from compacting and rotting. Make sure the grass has not gone to seed before spreading clippings on the garden, or you will end up with grass growing in the garden.
Leaves	Shredded leaves are best; apply 4 inches deep in summer. If you have only unshredded leaves, mix with wood chips or straw to keep them from compacting into a soggy mess. For winter mulch, apply 6 inches of shredded leaves, or 8 to 10 inches of unshredded leaves mixed with straw or wood chips.
Manure	Use only thoroughly composted manure as mulch; fresh manure may burn plants, and also smells bad. Apply 2 to 3 inches deep.
Newspaper	Black and white sheets are safest; although most printers no longer

use lead-based color inks, stick with black and white anyway. Lay 6 to 8 sheets thick. Cover with soil to hold papers in place and to hide them. Add nitrogen fertilizer to soil also. Newspaper will decompose in about a year, but you will still find clumps of it in the soil.

Peat moss *Not* recommended as mulch. May draw moisture from soil, repels water when it is dry, and blows around when dry.

Pine needles Attractive but best used to mulch acid-loving plants. May lower soil pH after several years of use. Lay 2 to 4 inches deep. Also burn readily when very dry.

Salt hay Adds trace minerals to soil and stays loose and light—does not pack down. Apply 2 to 3 inches deep.

Sawdust Apply 2 inches deep. Sawdust from pine and other soft woods increases soil acidity; best used around acid-loving plants. Add nitrogen fertilizer to soil before spreading sawdust. May blow away when dry, or form surface crust when drying out after being wet.

Stone Best used in areas where it is left in place permanently. Small stones are usually laid 1 to 2 inches deep over a layer of black plastic. Larger stones may be set individually, close together, around trees or between permanent beds. Stone is helpful in cool weather, when it warms the ground and releases heat stored during the day slowly at night, protecting tender plants. Also conserves soil moisture and keeps down weeds.

Straw Not a very attractive mulch for an ornamental garden, but effective when laid 8 to 10 inches deep (it will compact to half that depth in time). If tilled into soil in fall it will add organic matter as it decomposes over winter.

There are a couple of points to bear in mind in order to make the most of mulches. If you mulch with any kind of wood product—sawdust, shredded bark, wood chips—it is important to add nitrogen to the soil as well, because these materials take nitrogen from the soil as they decompose. If you mulch with grass clippings from your lawn, spread them in thin layers so they can dry out, and gradually build to the depth you need. If you lay down too deep a layer of fresh grass clippings they will pack down and rot into a slimy, smelly mess.

One organic material I would not advise using as a mulch is peat moss. Peat moss is difficult to moisten after it dries out, and when dry it can actually draw moisture out of the soil like a wick, and lose it to evaporation. When dry, peat moss will also repel rainwater, causing the water to run off the garden instead of soaking in. Peat also blows around when it is dry, and may not stay where you put it. Peat moss is a good source of organic matter for the garden, although there is now some concern, particularly in Europe, about depleting supplies in the ancient bogs where it was formed, as there will be no new supplies in our lifetime. If you decide to use peat in your garden, till it into the soil.

Pinching and Deadheading

Two important techniques for flower gardeners are pinching and deadheading.

Many plants with a branching growth habit can be encouraged to grow bushier when the growing tip is pinched off one or more times as the plants grow. Pinching out the tip stimulates dormant buds in leaf axils or farther down the stem to grow into side branches. The result is a fuller, bushier plant. Plants that benefit from pinching include chrysanthemums, marigolds, nicotiana, asters, summer phlox, and snapdragons.

Pinching off the flowers of basil, coleus, and other plants whose leaves are their most

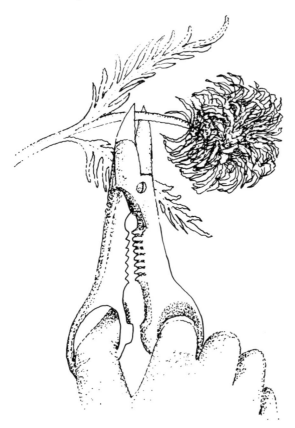

Deadhead most branching plants right above the nearest set of leaves.

important feature will help hold the leaves in good condition for the longest possible time. Eventually these plants will bloom anyway, but pinching off buds as soon as you see them does delay flowering for a while.

For some show or commercial plants, such as dahlias and carnations, some of the flowering stems are pinched off to channel the plant's energy into producing one or a few bigger blossoms.

Deadheading is picking off faded flowers. It can prolong the blooming period of many, many flowers. Deadheading is particularly effective for annuals, whose mission is to flower and produce seeds in a single growing season. If old flowers are picked off before they set seeds, the plants will keep on producing more flowers. Many annuals will bloom all summer and right up until frost if you deadhead them regularly.

Pinch off the dead flowers between your thumb and forefinger, or use pruning shears for stems that are thick, woody, or wiry, or flower snips for tiny flowers and delicate stems. In most cases it is best to pinch or cut right above the nearest set of leaves, so you don't leave a lot of headless flower stems sticking up from the plants. Not all plants follow this rule, at least not right away. Cosmos, for example, blooms in clusters of three successive flowers. After the first flower blooms, two new buds will form on either side of it, immediately below the old flower. The best way to deadhead is to cut the first blossom right below the head, then cut back to the next set of leaves after the second and third flowers in the group have bloomed. As you get to know plants you will learn how they bloom and where they send out new flowers.

In the case of plants that have a lot of small flowers that are too time-consuming to pick off by hand, such as sweet alyssum or threadleaf coreopsis, you can cut back the plants with flower shears when the first flush of bloom subsides, and they will rebloom.

Although I do not often recommend particular products, I have found two types of flower shears to be especially useful in the garden. One is a set of little snips with blades just one and one-half inches long, which I have found to be ideal for deadheading pansies and other delicate-stemmed plants. The other tool is a pair of shears that look very much like household scissors, with four-inch blades. The particular tools I use are made by Fiskars.

However you do it, by hand or with clipping tools, deadheading is time-consuming. But it is also a most rewarding activity. Regular deadheading keeps plants looking neat, and coaxes the maximum amount of bloom from them. It is well worth the time it takes.

Special Care for Bulbs

Although the focus of this book is on annuals and herbaceous perennials, most of us have bulbs, as well, in our gardens. In spring most garden centers sell bulb plants in pots with buds already set, for us to take home and enjoy. Most of these bulb plants—the hardy ones, at least, such as narcissus and crocus—can be planted out in the garden to bloom in subsequent years. They may fail to bloom the first year after planting out, since the bulbs are often exhausted by the forcing process they underwent before you bought them, but they usually build their strength and perform normally after the first year in the garden. Because most flower gardeners grow at least some bulbs, a few words on their care are in order here.

If you grow bulbs, especially hardy spring-blooming bulbs like daffodils, tulips, and crown imperials, you will be tempted to cut back the floppy, not terribly attractive leaves when the plants finish blooming. This is a temptation to avoid at all cost. Bulb foliage must be left in place to mature in order to nourish the bulb so it can produce flowers again next year. Leave the foliage alone until it yellows and dries, or leave it for at least six weeks after the end of flowering. In the old days, gardeners with time on their hands (or hired help) used to braid the long leaves of narcissus and daffodils to make the plants look a bit less shabby as the foliage ripened. These days it is simpler to simply plant annuals among the bulbs to camouflage the foliage. Be careful when planting not to damage the bulbs. You can also gather bunches of leaves together, fold them over and fasten with rubber bands to make them less conspicuous.

The potted bulbs you buy in early spring will have to be held over the summer and planted out in the garden in fall. After the plants finish blooming, continue to water when the soil becomes dry, to allow the foliage to grow. You can move the pots of leaves to a bright window in the basement, if you have one, or other sunny, out-of-the-way place. When the foliage starts to die back, six to eight weeks after the flowers have gone, you can taper off the watering. Cut off the dead leaves and let the soil dry out. If necessary, water lightly or mist thoroughly once a month or so to keep the bulbs from shrivelling. Plant them out at the normal bulb planting time for your area in autumn.

Controlling Pests and Diseases

It is true that healthy plants are less likely to suffer damage from pests and diseases than weak, sickly plants; scientific studies have proven it. It is also true that the best way to control pests and diseases is to prevent them in the first place. The gardener's most important lines of defense against garden thugs are to maintain plants in healthy condition and to take preventive measures against pests and diseases.

Maintaining healthy plants has been the subject of this chapter, so follow the recommendations in the preceding pages. Build your soil every year with compost or other organic matter, to provide the best possible growing medium for plants. Make sure there is an adequate supply of nutrients available for plants, but do not overfeed them. Overfertilizing stimulates fast, weak growth that is extremely susceptible to pest damage. Water plants when they need it, but do not overwater. Plants stressed by too much or too little moisture will be weakened.

Prevention will be the next topic of consideration. Although there is no way short of a chemical blitzkrieg to keep pests and diseases from invading your garden, there are several things you can do to help your plants withstand the damage when they do attack.

First and foremost, practice good sanitation. Simply keep the garden clean. Keep up with the weeding, and pick up dead leaves, flowers, and other trash that falls to the ground. Plant debris provides excellent hiding places for pests to overwinter and lay their eggs, as well as sites for disease organisms to take hold.

You can spread disease organisms from one plant to another just by working in the garden, so be careful. Do not work in the garden immediately after rain, when plants are still wet; harmful organisms may be transferred in the water on the leaves. Don't smoke in the garden; if you smoke at all, wash your hands before working around your plants. If you

must remove diseased or pest-infested parts of plants, place the debris in a plastic bag and put it in the trash. Do not put these damaged plant materials on the compost pile. Wash your hands when you finish, and sterilize any tools you have used. Actually, it is best to sterilize the tool after each cut. Dip tools in a solution of one part liquid chlorine bleach to nine parts water.

Do not crowd plants together when planting. Plants need sufficient room to develop properly if they are to remain vigorous, and good air circulation is also important, particularly for disease prevention. Mixed plantings also have fewer problems than entire beds or large blocks of a single type of plant.

If you tend to experience the same problems year after year, choose plants that are not usually prone to those problems, or plant resistant varieties. For example, if your zinnias always seem to get mildew, which can happen in cool, humid climates, seek out varieties bred for resistance to it, such as the Pulcino or Sun hybrids. Putting disease-susceptible plants in a different part of the garden each time you plant them may also help to reduce disease problems, by not allowing soilborne disease organisms to build up concentrated populations.

As you gain experience you will learn when to expect annual onslaughts of pests like Japanese beetles, that come every year. Keeping a garden journal is an immensely valuable memory aid. Major pest populations tend to arrive in the garden around the same time each year. If you know when to expect the invaders, you may be able to schedule plantings to avoid the worst of the siege, planting earlier or later so plants are not at the most critical stage of growth when the pests show up.

Keep a close watch on the garden throughout the growing season, and take action whenever you notice the first signs of pests or disease. Examine plants carefully, checking the leaf axils, undersides of leaves, growing tips, and flower buds for evidence of damage, insects, or their eggs. Problems are easiest to solve in their early stages, before the pest population assumes major proportions or disease spreads to several plants.

The safest approach is to use natural and plant-based controls that break down quickly after they are applied and do not linger in the environment. One of the most useful products I've found is insecticidal soap (from Safer or Ringer). It has proven very effective in my garden against aphids, whiteflies, flea beetles, and other small pests, and it does not seem to harm birds, bees, or butterflies. Sticky traps suspended among plants are effective against aphids and especially, whiteflies. These insects are attracted by the bright yellow color of the traps, and become stuck on the adhesive coating. When the trap is covered with bugs, it is discarded.

Plant-based insecticides include rotenone, pyrethrum, ryania, neem, and sabadilla. Use these botanical poisons as a last resort, because they kill beneficial insects along with pests. Diatomaceous earth controls soft-bodied pests, and *Bacillus thuringiensis* (sold as Bt or Dipel) is effective against cabbage worms and other caterpillars. If you use diatomaceous earth, buy a brand intended for horticultural use rather than the type sold for use in swimming pool filters. If Japanese beetles are a perennial problem for you, use milky spore disease (sold under the trade name Doom) to kill the grubs that winter over in your lawn. Pheromone traps can be helpful in controlling adult beetles, but do not place them in or immediately outside your garden, or they will actually lure more beetles to the garden.

Most of these organic controls must be reapplied after rain, but the extra effort seems a small price to pay for the peace of mind they afford.

If slugs and earwigs cause significant damage to your plants, you may wish to forgo mulching your beds and borders. Organic mulches offer ideal hiding places for these nocturnal invaders. Set out bait or traps to catch them, and empty the traps every day. Slugs can be lured with saucers of beer sunk into the ground with the rim even with the soil surface, or you can sprinkle them with salt. I have a real aversion to the monster slugs I see in my garden, and must confess to using slug pellets (which are not organic but which are very effective) occasionally to control them in seasons when they are particularly numerous. Sprinkling them with salt causes a slow death that is just too gruesome to watch, and leaves behind little piles of slug mush where the unfortunate creatures expire.

You can trap earwigs by giving them cozy places to hide out during the day. Placing rolled up newspapers on the ground in the garden works. Another method is to crumple a sheet of paper and put it in a tin can. Place the can upside down on a short stick, close to the plants that are suffering the worst damage. The earwigs will climb up into the paper during daylight hours. In the morning, collect your paper traps (either kind) and burn them, dump the contents into a small can of kerosene, or seal them inside plastic bags and put them in the garbage.

It is a good idea, too, to familiarize yourself with the beneficial insects in your garden—the helpful predators that eat the pests. Learn to recognize ladybugs, praying mantids, green lacewings, and other allies. If you spot them in your garden, leave them alone and consider yourself lucky. You can also purchase beneficial insects by mail to release into your garden.

As far as diseases are concerned, prevention is the best weapon, as described earlier. If you notice disease symptoms as you make your garden rounds, immediately remove the affected part of the plant. If more symptoms develop, pull up the entire plant and put it in the trash. Never put diseased plant material on the compost pile; even a hot pile will not get hot enough to destroy all pathogens. Sulfur sprays can help control fungus and mildew problems before they really take hold in the garden. You can use chemical fungicides and other products if you wish, but I prefer not to use them in my own garden.

A Guide to Common Garden Pests

Pest	Description and Symptoms	Controls
Aphids	Tiny, light green, dark green, or black bugs, with or without wings, gather on stems and under leaves. Leaves turn yellow and curl up.	Insecticidal soap, sticky traps, lacewing larvae, rotenone, pyrethrum, sabadilla.
Earwigs	Shiny dark brown beetles about 3/4 inch long, with pincers in back. Chew holes in leaves and flowers, may burrow inside flowers.	Insecticidal soap, traps.
Flea beetles	Tiny black insects, jump like fleas when disturbed. Leaves become full of tiny holes.	Diatomaceous earth, pyrethrum, rotenone, sabadilla.
Japanese beetles	Copper-winged flying beetled with metallic green heads, about 1/2 inch long. Chew holes in leaves, eventually skeletonizing them. Flowers are chewed and turn brown.	Milky spore disease to kill grubs in lawn. Pyrethrum, rotenone, pheromone traps for adult beetles.
Mealybugs	Fuzzy white blobs like tiny cotton balls in leaf axils and along stems.	Insecticidal soap, lacewing larvae; for small colonies, touch each blob with cotton swab dipped in rubbing alcohol.
Mites	Tiny, nearly invisible insects leave fine webbing over leaves and stems. Leaves eventually yellow, dry, and curl up.	Insecticidal soap, predatory mites, lacewing larvae, pyrethrum, rotenone, sulfur fungicide.
Nematodes	Very tiny worms in soil, attack roots and cause swellings and deformities. Plants are stunted, pale, sickly, and wilted.	Beneficial nematodes. Maintain high organic matter content in soil.

Pest	Description and Symptoms	Controls
Scale	Bumpy, scaly patches on stems and bark of shrubs and trees.	Insecticidal soap, horticultural oil sprays, ladybugs, lacewing larvae, pyrethrum, sabadilla.
Slugs	Look like snails without shells. Chew ragged holes in leaves, leave behind silvery, slimy trails.	Diatomaceous earth or wood ashes around plants or perimeter of garden, traps.
Thrips	Tiny brownish insects resembling minuscule, dark-colored threads. Flowers are streaked with brown and may wither.	Insecticidal soap, ladybugs, lacewing larvae, pyrethrum, sabadilla, sulfur.
Whiteflies	Tiny white flies; when plant is disturbed they fly around it like a cloud of snowflakes. Leaves turn yellow and dry, black mold grows on leaves, leaves drop.	Insecticidal soap, sticky traps, lacewing larvae, pyrethrum, ryania.

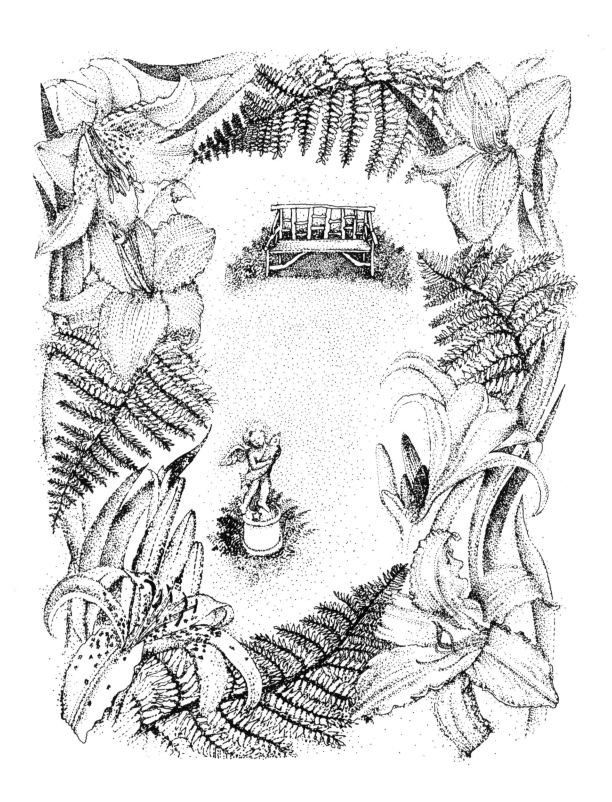

Chapter Five

A Concise Guide to Common Plants

This chapter is a guide to many of the plants that are widely available in local nurseries and garden centers. A brief description of each plant is given, including the plant's overall shape and texture, the color of its flowers and when they bloom, and the shape and color of its leaves. You will also find information of each plant's cultural requirements, and suggestions for using the plant in the garden. This guide is intended to be used as a quick reference, and is set up in an easy-to-use format. Most plants are listed in alphabetical order by their botanical names. Herbs, however, are listed by their common names, which are most familiar to most of us. If you do not know the botanical name of a particular plant, consult the Index of Common Plant Names in the back of the book, immediately preceding the general index. Then you can proceed to look up the plant in this chapter. For more detailed information on specific plants you can consult a good book on growing annuals or perennials; several are listed in Recommended Reading, which follows the Glossary.

As explained in Chapter One, for our purposes here, the terms full sun, partial shade, and shade can be defined as follows:

Full sun is a location receiving six or more hours of direct, unobstructed sunlight per day;

partial shade means two to six hours of good sun, with light, dappled shade the rest of the day;

shade indicates a location that receives up to two hours of sun, or light, dappled shade all day.

If your garden is shaded by a building for most of the day, the shade cast is more dense than the shade cast by a tree with a relatively light canopy. If you are gardening in such conditions, I recommend you consult a book on gardening in shade.

Light needs for individual plants are given in order of each plant's preference. That is, if full sun to partial shade is recommended, the plant prefers full sun but will also perform adequately in partial shade.

Some plants need a soil that is humusy, or rich in organic matter. For information on how to boost the organic matter content of your soil, see Chapter Four. Chapter One explains how to judge whether your soil drains quickly or slowly, and how to improve the drainage ability of dense, slow-draining soil.

If you are unsure what I mean when I recommend moist but well-drained soil for plants, read The Best Site for a Garden, in Chapter One.

The term average moisture refers to conditions in which the soil dries out somewhat between rainfalls or waterings, but does not get so dry that plants wilt. In some gardens average moisture means the garden must get an inch of water a week. For the best way to tell when it is time to water your garden, see Watering, in Chapter Four.

At the end of each plant entry, under Comments, you will find information on the

Understanding a plant's basic form will help you use it effectively in the garden. Low, mounded plants like impatiens (top left) look best in the foreground. Branching plants such as nicotiana (top right) add mass to the middle ground. Spiky plants like daylily (bottom left) add vertical line. Use trailers like vinca (bottom right) to edge containers.

plant's function in the garden, for example, whether it works best for edging, or in the middle of the garden, or as background. I have also noted special qualities the plant possesses, such as whether it has a particularly long blooming period, or the flowers are good for cutting.

Use this chapter as a guide when selecting plants for the garden; you might even want to carry the book along to the garden center with you when you buy plants. Then consult this chapter again for advice on planting and caring for the plants you chose.

Achillea
Yarrow
Achillea species
Perennial

Achillea's flat-topped clusters of tiny flowers are carried on tall, slender stems above a clump of feathery, ferny foliage that is rather grayish green in color. Flowers can be rich, golden yellow, light yellow, white, pink, or red, depending upon the species or cultivar. Plants have an upright, branched shape when in bloom, and an airy look; when not in bloom the leaves grow in a rather low, more or less mounded form.

Blooming time: Midsummer; some continue blooming until fall

Height: 1½ to 4 feet, depending on species or cultivar

Spacing: 1 to 1½ feet

Light: Full sun

Soil: Well-drained, loamy soil preferred, but plants adapt to a range of conditions

Moisture: Average; tolerates dry soil

Comments: A handsome plant for the middle of the garden. Achillea is easy to grow and tolerates hot, dry conditions—an excellent plant for seaside gardens. Plants have a long blooming period for a perennial, often flowering for a month or more. The flowers dry well.

Ageratum

Flossflower

Ageratum houstonianum

Annual

Clusters of small, short-stemmed, powder puff flowers in violet-blue, pink, or white adorn these small plants. The flowers sit just above the broadly oval, light to medium green leaves. Plants have a low, bushy form.

Blooming time: All summer

Height: 6 to 12 inches

Spacing: Set dwarf varieties 6 to 9 inches apart, taller varieties 12 inches apart

Light: Full sun to light shade; does best with some afternoon shade in hot climates

Soil: Well-drained, average fertility

Moisture: Average

Comments: An easy-to-grow plant for the front of the garden, or edging. Also nice for containers and windowboxes. Ageratum cannot tolerate any frost; do not plant it out until all danger of frost is past in spring.

Alcea

Hollyhock

Alcea rosea

Short-lived perennial grown as annual or biennial

Stately hollyhocks are noted for their tall spikes of large, ruffled flowers in many shades of red and pink, also white or yellow. The saucer-shaped flowers are carried along the upper portion of the thick, straight stems, above large, broadly oval or lobed leaves. Plants are upright and vertical, not bushy or branched.

Blooming time: Early to late summer

Height: Standard varieties, 4 to 9 feet; dwarf varieties 2 to 3 feet

Spacing: 1½ to 2 feet, depending on mature size

Light: Full sun

Soil: Fertile, moist but well-drained

Moisture: Average

Comments: A good plant for the back of the garden or for screening. Hollyhocks are easy to grow but susceptible to fungus disease; remove affected plants immediately. Plants may self-sow.

Amaranthus

Amaranthus caudatus, Love-lies-bleeding

A. tricolor, Joseph's Coat

Annual

Love-lies-bleeding, or tasselflower, has long, deep red flower spikes; Joseph's coat is grown for its colorful leaves of red, yellow, orange, bronze, and/or chocolate brown. Both plants have a branched shape, and oval leaves. Love-lies-bleeding is a large, rather coarse-textured plant; Joseph's coat is more compact.

Blooming time: Summer
Height: 1 to 4 feet, depending on species
Spacing: 1½ to 2 feet
Light: Full sun
Soil: Average, well-drained. Joseph's coat has less colorful leaves in rich soil.
Moisture: Average
Comments: Amaranthus is easy to grow, but transplants best when young. Handle carefully when transplanting into the garden. Both types grow best in warm weather.

Grow amaranthus in the middle ground of a garden of large plants, or in the back of a garden of small plants.

Anemone
Japanese Anemone
Anemone ✕hybrida
Perennial

Elegant, five-petaled flowers about 2 inches across (the "petals" are actually sepals) of pink, rose, or white, with a light golden center bloom on tall, branched stems, above a low mound of divided or compound, deeply toothed green leaves.

Blooming time: Late summer to early autumn
Height: 1½ to 5 feet, depending on variety
Spacing: 1 to 2 feet
Light: Partial shade to full sun
Soil: Fertile, moist but well-drained
Moisture: Best with even moisture
Comments: Lovely plants for the fall garden, Japanese anemones are a wonderful companion to mums in purple and yellow shades, or a perfect successor to summer perennials.

Plant Japanese anemones in the middle or background of the garden, in a spot that is sheltered from strong winds.

Japanese anemone is not hardy in the far North.

Antirrhinum
Snapdragon
Antirrhinum majus
Perennial usually grown as an annual

Snapdragons offer spikes of beak-shaped flowers in shades of pink, red, purple, yellow, orange, and white, on upright plants with narrow green leaves. The plants have a strong vertical line that is somewhat softened by the horizontal leaves.

Blooming time: Summer; snapdragons usually rebloom if cut back after flowering
Height: 7 inches to 3 feet, depending on variety
Spacing: 6 to 12 inches
Light: Full sun; will tolerate partial shade
Soil: Moist but well-drained
Moisture: Average
Comments: Easy-to-grow plants for the middle of the garden; dwarf varieties work well in the front of the garden or in containers. The tallest-growing varieties can be used in the background of a garden of smaller plants.

Snapdragons are hardy in warm climates but grow best in cool weather. They are susceptible to fungus disease, so it is best to start with new plants each year. Pinch back the plants when young to encourage them to branch.

Snapdragons make good cut flowers.

Aquilegia
Columbine
Aquilegia species
Perennial

The graceful, spurred blossoms of columbine come in shades of purple, blue, pink, rose,

*W*hen buying plants for the garden, pay attention to the environment in which they are growing at the garden center. Plants coming from a greenhouse or other protected location must be hardened-off before you plant them outdoors. See Chapter Three for details.

*O*ne indication of a good garden center is plants displayed in conditions similar to those they prefer in the garden. Plants for shady gardens are best kept out of full sun in the garden center.

*P*lant shopping is simplified when the garden center clearly marks which plants are best in sun and which ones can tolerate shade.

*L*ook for sun-loving plants in full sun (and watered when necessary) at your local garden center or nursery.

*I*f you buy plants already in bloom, like these impatiens, they will provide instant color in the garden, but they may drop some blossoms as they become accustomed to the garden environment.

*I*t is generally best to look for plants with lots of buds but few fully open flowers, like the browallia shown here. See Chapter Three for more information.

*P*lants are not generally sold in undivided flats. Most are grown in individual cell packs (also called six packs or market packs) in which each plant gets its own compartment. The cell packs are sold individually or in full flats.

*C*ell packs come in several sizes, but none are meant to hold mature plants. The plants in these packs are still healthy, but they need to be transplanted to more spacious quarters promptly or their growth will begin to suffer.

*S*ome growers prefer to use 4-inch round pots, like the ones holding these dusty miller plants.

*T*hese 8-inch pots are large enough to allow geraniums to grow to their full size. If you buy plants this big, handle them carefully during transplanting, and try to retain as much as possible of the original soil ball around the roots.

*L*arger plants farther along in their development are sold in plastic pots of various sizes. The 4-inch square pots shown here are very widely used.

*T*his photograph and the two that follow show three
ways to use impatiens. Here, masses of impatiens planted
behind a low dry stone wall frame the interesting log
house and separate it from the lawn.

*T*he white impatiens here seem
almost to have overflowed the container and taken root in the ground
nearby. The effect is rather like a
fountain and pool of flowers.

*I*nstead of planting the
typical ring of impatiens
around the base of a tree,
this gardener built a two-
tiered bed, accommodating
more flowers and allowing
all of them to be seen
easily.

*P*ortulaca, or rose moss, makes a brilliant edging for a sunny bed or border. The plants can tolerate poor, dry soil, as long as they get lots of sun.

Bottom Right
*R*udbeckia is a tough, easy-to-grow plant for a sunny garden. It can withstand both hot and cold weather, as well as dry soil, and blooms over a long period.

Bottom Left
*C*hoosing plants with a gradation of heights, as this gardener did, with the shortest plants in the front of the garden and the tallest plants in the back, creates visual depth and allows all the flowers to be readily visible.

*J*apanese anemone is an outstanding plant for end-of-summer to early autumn bloom, and makes a welcome change from the ubiquitous chrysanthemums.

*T*all cannas add height to the center or back of a summer garden. The bold-textured plants with their large leaves and strong stems have a tropical look.

*C*ombining a variety of forms and textures adds interest to the garden. This planting mixes white cone-flowers with airy spikes of blue salvia, the bushy, rich red foliage of coleus, and the glowing golden daisy flowers of rudbeckia.

*T*hyme has a creeping habit and can be planted as a fragrant ground-cover in sunny areas that do not get a lot of foot traffic.

*H*ostas are outstanding for shady places; they are easy to grow and come in a host of sizes, in shades of green from chartreuse to blue-green, and assorted white and gold variegation patterns.

A fine-textured, silvery artemisia lights up and softens the surrounding green foliage in this garden.

red, yellow, and white, some bicolored, and are carried on slender stems above a clump of medium green leaves with scalloped edges. The plants have a low, bushy form when not in bloom.

Blooming time: Late spring to early summer
Height: 1 to 3 feet, depending on species or variety
Spacing: 12 to 15 inches
Light: Partial to light shade; tolerates full sun in cool northern gardens
Soil: Moist but well-drained, average fertility
Moisture: Average
Comments: Columbines are absolutely lovely in the front or middle of a shady garden; the leaves are attractive even when plants are not blooming. Nonhybrid forms will self-sow and colonize an area. Otherwise, plants are short-lived and need to be replaced every few years. Deadheading to prevent plants from setting seeds may prolong their life.

Columbines are native to mountain regions and most can tolerate some heat and dryness.

Artemisia

Artemisia species
Perennial

These useful plants are grown for their lacy, silvery, foliage, which is aromatic. Some species, such as Silver King artemisia (*Artemisia ludoviciana*), are upright and bushy; others, such as *A. schmidtiana* 'Silver Mound' form low, dense mounds of leaves.

Blooming time: Although grown for their foliage, artemisias do produce small yellow or white flowers in mid to late summer. Plants generally look best when the flowers are removed, although some gardeners like to leave them on the plants.

Height: 6 inches to 3 feet, depending upon species or variety
Spacing: 10 inches to 1½ feet, depending on species or variety
Light: Full sun
Soil: Well-drained, sandy, poor to average fertility
Moisture: Artemisias tolerate drought, and fare poorly in wet, humid conditions
Comments: Easy-to-grow foliage plants for sunny gardens, artemisias are immensely useful in flower beds and borders, where their cool silver leaves can help to tone down brilliant colors and sharp contrasts. Plant small artemisias in the front of the garden, taller ones in the middle ground.

In very cold climates artemisias can be grown as annuals.

If the plants start to look ratty in hot, humid weather, cut them back and they will regrow.

Aster

Aster species
Perennial

Hardy perennial asters belong to this genus; the botanical name of the China aster is *Callistephus.* Perennial asters have daisylike flowers in shades of lavender, blue, purple, red, rose, pink, and white on branched plants with medium to deep green leaves. Asters have a loose form, and can look rather dishevelled and weedy.

Blooming time: Midsummer into fall
Height: 15 inches to 4 feet, depending on species or variety
Spacing: 1 to 2 feet
Light: Full sun
Soil: Asters will grow in just about any soil, but well-drained, fertile soil is ideal

Moisture: These plants need plenty of water; keep them evenly moist but not soggy

Comments: Easy to grow and adaptable, asters are outstanding in autumn gardens, mixing well with chrysanthemums. All they want in order to thrive is abundant sunshine and water.

Plant asters near the middle of the garden, the tallest types in the background. Asters work best in informal or naturalistic gardens; their appearance is not neat and controlled enough for a formal bed or border.

Asters can be troubled by mildew in humid climates. Generous spacing that allows good air circulation may help. The plants may self-sow.

Astilbe

False Spirea
Astilbe species
Perennial

Gardeners love astilbe for their fluffy plumes or spires of tiny blossoms in shades of red, rose, pink, or white. The flowers are carried on slender stems above divided, ferny, dark green or bronzy foliage. The plants appear bushy when in bloom; the foliage grows in a low, loose but neat clump.

Blooming time: Early to late summer, depending on species or variety

Height: 1 to 3½ feet, depending on species or variety

Spacing: 10 to 15 inches

Light: Partial shade is best

Soil: Moist but well-drained, especially in winter when plants are dormant; humusy; fertile. Astilbe can tolerate full sun in very moist soils.

Moisture: Plants like plenty of moisture

Comments: The delicate flowers of astilbe are exquisite in partly shady beds and borders, where the colors positively glow in the soft light.

Position dwarf varieties of astilbe in the foreground, taller types in the middle of the garden.

Basil

Ocimum basilicum
Annual

This classic culinary herb is grown for its savory leaves, which may be either green or purple, oval and smooth-edged or with deeply toothed or ruffled edges, in a range of sizes. Numerous varieties are available. There are also varieties with differently scented leaves redolent of lemon, cinnamon, and licorice. Green-leaved varieties produce small spikes of tiny white flowers, purple varieties have pink flowers, but none of the flowers are very decorative. The plants have a bushy, branched form, except for some dwarf varieties that grow in the shape of a low mound.

Blooming time: Mid to late summer, but flowers are best picked off

Height: 1 to 3 feet

Spacing: 10 to 12 inches

Light: Full sun

Soil: Moist but well-drained, fertile

Moisture: Average

Comments: Basil is easy to grow in containers or in the front or middle ground of sunny gardens. The purple varieties are especially ornamental; they are lovely with pink or yellow flowers.

Pinch back plants to encourage bushiness. Pinching out the flower buds as soon as they form in the growing tips and leaf axils will postpone blooming and retain best leaf quality for a longer time.

Basil needs warm weather to grow well; do not plant it out until all danger of frost is past in spring and the soil has warmed.

Begonia

Begonia ×semperflorens-cultorum, Wax Begonia
B. ×hiemalis, Reiger Begonia
Tender perennial grown as annual

Wax begonias bear small flowers in shades of pink, red, and white on compact, bushy plants with wide, fleshy, green or bronzy leaves. Reiger begonias are somewhat larger, with larger, deep green leaves and ruffled flowers in bright red, orange, yellow, or pink.
Blooming time: All summer
Height: Wax begonias, 6 to 12 inches; Reiger begonias about 1 foot
Spacing: 6 to 8 inches for wax begonias; 9 to 12 inches for Reigers
Light: Partial shade. Wax begonias also tolerate sun or deeper shade; in sun they need lots of moisture, and in more than partial shade they will not bloom as well. Reiger begonias will bloom in partial to full shade, especially if the plants have already set buds when you buy them.
Soil: Moist, fertile, well-drained
Moisture: Plants need even moisture
Comments: Classic bedding plants, wax begonias are perfect for edging or containers and windowboxes. Plants with bronze leaves like more sun than green-leaved varieties.

Reiger begonias have traditionally been grown as winter-blooming greenhouse plants, but can now be found in garden centers for use as summer flowers in shady gardens or containers. Treat them as annuals.

Neither type of begonia can tolerate cold. Do not plant them outdoors until the soil has warmed in spring, and nights are no longer cold.

Brachycome

Swan River Daisy
Brachycome iberidifolia
Annual

Daisylike flowers of lavender-blue, about an inch across, on branched, bushy plants with narrow, needlelike leaves. The thin-stemmed plants have a delicate, airy texture.
Blooming time: All summer
Height: 8 to 12 inches
Spacing: 6 to 8 inches
Light: Full sun
Soil: Well-drained, of average fertility
Moisture: Can tolerate dry soil
Comments: Swan River daisy is an excellent plant for container gardens, windowboxes, and hanging baskets. It also makes a charming edging or front-of-the-garden plant. Although the plant likes soil on the dry side, it grows best in cool weather. If blooming slows considerably during hot weather, cut back the plants by about one-third, and they should put forth new growth and a fresh crop of flowers.

Browallia

Browallia speciosa
Annual

Browallia bears star-shaped, violet-blue flowers about 2 inches across on branching plants with small, oval leaves of deep green. The compact plants have a bushy form. There is also a white-flowered variety.
Blooming time: Summer
Height: 9 to 14 inches
Spacing: 10 inches

Light: Full sun to partial shade
Soil: Moist but well-drained; of average fertility, not too rich
Moisture: Browallia needs abundant moisture
Comments: An underused plant, browallia is delightful for edging beds and borders, or for growing in pots, windowboxes, and hanging baskets. The plant grows best in fairly warm weather.

Brunnera
Siberian Bugloss
Brunnera macrophylla
Perennial

Sprays of small, sky blue forget-me-not flowers with yellow centers are carried on slender stems above large, coarse-textured, heart-shaped leaves of medium green. The leaves grow in a bushy clump and remain attractive all season if plants receive sufficient moisture.
Blooming time: Mid to late spring
Height: 1 to 1½ feet; the leaves grow approximately 9 to 12 inches tall
Spacing: 12 to 15 inches
Light: Partial shade, shade, or full sun
Soil: Brunnera prefers deep, moist but well-drained soil with lots of organic matter, but adapts to a range of soils
Comments: A handsome, easy-to-grow plant to put near the front of beds and borders. Brunnera will spread from year to year after it becomes established; if the young plants become a problem, pull them up and transplant or give them to gardening friends.

Brunnera is especially handsome planted around shrubs. Some gardeners find they prefer this plant to the true forget-me-not (*Myosotis*) because the leaves are more interesting and decorative.

Caladium
Elephant's Ear
C. ×hortulanum
Tender bulb

These exotic foliage plants bring a bold, tropical look and a splash of color to a shady garden or container. The plants grow from tubers, and in all but frost-free climates, they are grown as annual summer bedding plants. The large leaves are broad and lobed, somewhat like a heart or arrowhead shape, and thin-textured rather than stiff. Leaves are variegated green and white, green and pink, green and red, or red, pink, and green. They grow on long, graceful petioles.

Height: 1 to 1½ feet

Spacing: 9 to 12 inches

Light: Partial shade to shade

Soil: Moist but well-drained, fertile

Moisture: Even moisture is best

Comments: Caladiums are too big and flashy for some gardeners, but they do bring a welcome shot of bright color to shady areas, and work quite well when combined with white flowers and lots of green foliage. Plant them in the front of a shady bed or border, or in pots or mixed tub gardens.

The plants absolutely cannot tolerate cold, so do not set them outdoors until late spring (depending on where you live), when the weather is warm and nighttime temperatures have settled, no longer dropping below 50 degrees Fahrenheit.

Pull and discard the plants at the end of the season, or dig and store the tubers indoors over winter in a cool, dry place. Shake off excess dirt, and spread out the tubers so air can circulate among them.

Calendula

Pot Marigold
Calendula officinalis
Annual

Calendula produces golden yellow, orange, or cream-colored daisy flowers on bushy, branching plants with narrow, oblong, rather coarse-textured green leaves. Some varieties have full, double-petaled flowers.

Blooming time: Early summer to fall
Height: 1 to 2 feet
Spacing: 8 to 12 inches
Light: Full sun
Soil: Well-drained, average fertility
Moisture: Average
Comments: Plant these sunny flowers near the front or middle of the garden. They grow best in cool weather and can tolerate some frost; plant out in early spring, as soon as they become available. Gardeners in warm climates can plant calendula for winter flowers.

Calendulas are easy to grow and have herbal as well as decorative uses. The dried flower petals can be used as a substitute for saffron, to add color to rice dishes. Calendulas also make good cut flowers.

Callistephus

China Aster
Callistephus chinensis
Annual

These shaggy, many-petaled daisy flowers bloom in shades of blue, violet, rose, pink, red, and white on compact, branching plants. The flowers have a full, pompom shape.

Blooming time: Midsummer
Height: 6 inches to 1½ feet, depending on variety

Spacing: 10 to 15 inches
Light: Full sun is best, but will tolerate partial shade
Soil: Average fertility, moist but well-drained
Moisture: Average
Comments: China asters are usually sold in mixed-color assortments, with shades of purple and blue-violet the dominant colors.

Plant dwarf varieties as edging or in the front of borders, pots, or windowboxes; place taller varieties in the middle ground.

China asters can be susceptible to disease; choose disease-resistant varieties when possible. Do not crowd the plants; allow room for air to circulate among them. China asters cannot tolerate any frost, so do not plant them outdoors until all danger of frost is past.

The flowers are good for cutting.

Campanula

Bellflower
Campanula species
Perennial or biennial grown as annual

These charming, old-fashioned flowers are shaped like bells, and come in shades of violet and blue-violet, white, pink, and mauve. The plants are erect and branched, but not really bushy, with narrow to oblong leaves of medium to deep green, depending on the species.

Blooming time: Late spring to late summer, depending on species
Height: 1 to 4 feet, depending on species. The annual species, *Campanula medium*, grows 2 to 4 feet tall.
Spacing: 10 to 18 inches, depending on species
Light: Full sun to partial shade
Soil: Fertile, moist but well-drained, with neutral to mildly alkaline pH

Moisture: Average
Comments: Campanulas are lovely plants for the front or middle of the garden, depending on their size. They are favorites for cottage gardens.

You may also find them under the name of Canterbury bells or harebell.

Canna

Canna ✕ *generalis*
Tender bulb

These big plants boast large, flashy flowers in shades of red, rose, yellow, and orange, on tall, straight stalks above large, broad leaves.
Blooming time: Midsummer to early fall
Height: 3 to 6 feet, depending on variety
Spacing: 15 inches to 2 feet
Light: Full sun
Soil: Moist but well-drained, fertile, humusy
Moisture: Plants need to be watered thoroughly and regularly during dry weather
Comments: Big, bold cannas are difficult to combine with other garden flowers. Try them in an island bed or border by themselves, or massed in the back of the garden. Cannas are like exclamation points in the garden, not for those who like subtle, quiet effects.

Cannas need hot weather to grow well. Unless you live in a frost-free climate, dig the bulbs before the first fall frost, and store them indoors over winter. Warm-climate gardeners can grow cannas as perennials.

Celosia

Woolflower
Celosia cristata
Annual

A varied species, celosia offers flower heads in feathery plumes, loose spires, or a variety of bizarre curled, crested, and fan shapes, some resembling twisted corals, brains, or deformed rooster's combs. The flowers have traditionally come in bright, hot colors: reds, magenta, scarlet, rose, pink, orange, and yellow, but there are now also softer shades of gold, yellow, apricot, and cream, particularly among the plume type (which is often sold under the name *Celosia plumosa*). The plants are upright with a branching to bushy form and oval leaves.
Blooming time: All summer
Height: 6 inches to 2 feet, depending on variety
Spacing: 1 to 2 feet, depending on type. Smaller-growing varieties can be planted at the closer spacing; larger ones farther apart.
Light: Full sun
Soil: Any good garden soil
Moisture: Average
Comments: The traditional brilliant colors of celosia are difficult to mix with other flowers and are best surrounded with white flowers, silver-gray foliage like that of artemisia or dusty miller, or lots of green foliage. But newer, softer cultivars are easier to work with and can be quite pretty with other warm-toned flowers.

Use celosia in the front of the garden, taller types in the middle ground, or grow it in containers.

The flowers are good for cutting and drying.

The plants cannot tolerate cold, so do not plant them out in the garden until the soil has warmed in spring.

Chives

Allium schoenoprasum
Perennial

The ball-shaped, edible, purple-pink flowerheads of chives appear in spring, at the tips of the upright, slender, hollow green leaves that grow in a clump.

Blooming time: Late spring

Height: To 1½ feet

Spacing: 8 to 10 inches

Light: Full sun to partial shade

Soil: Average to fertile, well-drained

Comments: Chives are extremely easy to grow, and are valued by cooks for the mild onion flavor of their leaves and flowers. The clumps of leaves will expand over the years and need division periodically. Chives also grow well in pots, but they will need to be divided and replanted every year, in fall or early spring, unless you grow them in a large container where they will have room to spread out a bit.

A few clumps of chives can be decorative near the front of an informal garden, as well as useful in the kitchen.

Chrysanthemum

Chrysanthemum frutescens, Marguerite
C. ×morifolium, Garden Mum
C. ×superbum, Shasta Daisy
Perennial

Our familiar garden mums come in many warm shades: crimson, scarlet, maroon, orange, apricot, gold, bronze, yellow, pink, also purple and white, in a variety of flower forms from single daisies to full round pompons. Shasta daisies are classic daisy flowers, white with yellow centers. The smaller marguerites have dainty daisy flowers of white or yellow, about an inch across, with golden centers. Plants are branched and bushy; garden mums have lobed leaves; shasta daisies have elongated leaves with smooth or slightly notched edges; marguerites have finely divided, rather lacy-looking leaves.

Blooming time: Garden mums bloom from midsummer to autumn, depending on the variety; shasta daisies bloom in early to late summer; marguerites flower all summer if deadheaded regularly

Height: 1 to 3 feet

Spacing: 1 to 2 feet

Light: Full sun

Soil: Fertile, moist but well-drained

Moisture: Mums need even, abundant moisture; shasta daisies and marguerites are a bit less fussy, but are not very tolerant of drought

Comments: Garden mums require lots of work—division every year or two, and pinching back early in the season for the best blooms and bushy, nicely shaped plants. For plants to winter over, it is best to buy young plants early in the season; plants purchased in bloom in autumn will probably not winter over in the garden.

Despite their problems, mums are classics for fall gardens, and their warm, glowing earth tones combine well with asters. Plant them in the middle ground, or in containers.

Garden center mums are so inexpensive in autumn that many people buy them to use as decorative potted plants during the fall season, then discard them when they finish blooming.

Shasta daisies are less work to grow than hardy mums and are classic, long-stemmed flowers for cutting gardens. The smaller marguerites are wonderful in container gardens and windowboxes, and perform beautifully as long as they receive regular deadheading throughout the summer.

Botanists have reclassified shasta daisy into the genus *Leucanthemum,* and marguerites as *Argyranthemum,* but most suppliers still label both plants in the genus *Chrysanthemum.*

Cleome

Spider Flower
Cleome hasslerana
Annual

This rather amazing plant is among the tallest of annuals, growing up to 6 feet high in a single summer. Its distinctive flowers, with their long, waving stamens (that resemble the legs of the spiders children call "daddy long legs") are gathered into loose, round clusters at the tops of the tall, upright stems. Flowers come in shades of rose, pink, and purple, as well as white. The medium green leaves are deeply lobed and palm-shaped.

Blooming time: All summer

Height: 4 to 6 feet; plants will not be as tall when growing in containers or in less-than-optimum conditions

Spacing: 1 to 2 feet

Light: Full sun to partial shade

Soil: Average, well-drained

Moisture: Can tolerate dry soil, but not prolonged drought

Comments: These tall plants are extraordinarily striking when massed in the back of the garden, where they provide a strong vertical line. Or you can use spider flower to add height in the center or back of a tub garden of mixed flowers.

Transplant spider flowers with care; they do not transplant very well. They can be planted outdoors in spring, after the weather begins to warm but before all danger of frost is past. The plants may self-sow, but self-sown plants will not grow as large or vigorous as their parents.

The tall stems may need staking, especially if your garden is in a windy location. The flowers are good for cutting and add interest to summer bouquets and arrangements.

Coleus

Coleus hybrids
Tender perennial grown as annual

These branched, bushy plants are grown for their oval to lance-shaped leaves that come in various combinations of colors: green, chartreuse, red, maroon, white, pink, apricot, brown, and yellow. The leaves have toothed, scalloped, or frilled edges and a somewhat quilted texture. In summer the plants send up small spikes of little white or purple flowers which detract from their appearance and are best removed.

Blooming time: Mid to late summer

Height: 8 inches to 2 feet

Spacing: 8 to 12 inches, depending on variety; set smaller-growing plants at the closer spacing

Light: Partial shade is preferred, but coleus will also grow in full sun. In full shade the plants will be smaller and less full; in full sun the colors will not be as rich

Soil: Average; tolerates a range of soils

Moisture: Plants need even moisture, especially in dry weather

Comments: Coleus is a good source of color and mass in the front of a shady garden, or in the middle ground of a bed of small plants. It also grows well in pots.

The plants are tender, so do not plant them in the garden until all danger of frost is past. Pinch back the tips of young plants to encourage bushier plants. Pinch off flowers when they form. You will have to pinch at least once a week; the plants have a strong urge to bloom and will keep trying to produce new flower spikes. You may decide you like the flowers and can leave them in place.

You can take stem cuttings at the end of summer and root them in water, then pot them up to grow as houseplants in winter.

Coreopsis

Coreopsis species
Annual or perennial

The golden yellow to pale yellow daisy-like flowers can be single or double, depending upon the cultivar; the petals of some annual varieties have a deep red to brownish red base. The flowers bloom on tall, slender stems. Plants are upright and branched, bushy in some cases, with medium green leaves varying from lance-shaped to ferny to needle-like, depending on species.

Blooming time: All summer, if deadheaded regularly
Height: 8 inches to 3 feet
Spacing: 8 to 12 inches
Light: Full sun
Soil: Well-drained, of average fertility; will tolerate poor soil
Moisture: Average
Comments: Easy to grow, reliable plants for the front or middle of the garden. Coreopsis holds up well in hot weather, and tends to bloom best when planted close together. Most coreopsis have flowers of deep golden yellow, but one cultivar, Moonbeam, has soft yellow blossoms that look especially pretty with pink and blue flowers.

Warm-climate gardeners can grow annual coreopsis for winter flowers; the plants can tolerate cool weather.

The flowers are good for cutting.

Cosmos

Cosmos species
Annual

The golden-centered daisy flowers of crimson, rose, pink, and white (*Cosmos bipinnatus*) or scarlet, orange, gold, and yellow (*C. sulphureus*) are extraordinarily appealing in summer beds and borders. Cosmos foliage is finely divided and has a feathery appearance. The branching plants have a light, open texture and may look a bit weedy late in the season.

Blooming time: Midsummer until frost
Height: 2 to 5 feet, depending on variety and growing conditions
Spacing: 12 inches
Light: Full sun is best; also grows reasonably well in partial shade
Soil: Average fertility; good drainage is essential; tolerates poor soil
Moisture: Tolerates some drought
Comments: Cosmos is a wonderful, exuberant plant for the middle to the back of the garden, depending on the mature height of the cultivar. The flowers come in a handsome range of colors that combine beautifully with many other flowers.

Transplant carefully, and not until all danger of frost is past in spring.

The plants hold up well in hot weather, and the flowers are excellent for cutting.

The pink and white species of cosmos blooms in groups of three flowers. When deadheading the first blooms, cut them off immediately below the flowerhead; two new buds will then form below the cut. After these flowers fade, clip off the stems at the next pair of leaves when deadheading. Flowers of the yellow and orange species appear singly on long stems; cut back to the next pair of leaves when deadheading.

Dahlia

Dahlia cultivars
Tender bulb

These classic summer flowers come in a host of shapes from daisylike to ball-shaped, with petals in a variety of forms. The color range encompasses shades of red, rose, purple, pink, orange, salmon, and yellow, as well as white—all colors except blue. The flowers of some varieties are flushed or tipped with a second color. The branched, bushy plants have oval, sometimes compound green leaves with toothed edges. They grow from tuberous roots.

Blooming time: Early summer to frost; many are at their best in early autumn

Height: 1 to 6 feet, depending on variety

Spacing: 10 inches to 3 feet

Light: Full sun

Soil: Fertile, moist but well-drained, deeply dug and not too heavy

Moisture: Dahlias need abundant moisture, but not soggy conditions

Comments: Plant dahlias in the front, middle, or back of the garden, according to their mature size. Tall varieties will need staking.

The tubers cannot stand cold; do not plant out until after all danger of frost is past. Except in zone 9 and south, dig the tubers before the first frost and store indoors in a cool, dry place, or grow the plants as annuals. If you save the clusters of tubers, separate them and plant them individually the following spring.

The many dahlia varieties are classified into several distinct flower forms for exhibition purposes, such as cactus, pompon, mignon, collarette, peony, and decorative.

Dianthus

Garden Pinks

Dianthus species

Annual, biennial, or perennial

The perennial pinks most often found in garden centers, Allwood pink (*Dianthus ×allwoodii*), cheddar pink (*D. gratianopolitanus*), and grass pinks (*D. plumarius*), bear small disc-shaped flowers on slender upright stems; the petals have fringed or toothed edges. Perennial pinks come in many shades

of pink, rose, red, salmon, and white; many are bicolored. The low, mat-forming plants have grassy, gray- or blue-green leaves.

The flowers of sweet William (*Dianthus barbatus*) are gathered into clusters atop upright, branched plants 1 to 2 feet high; they come in many shades of pink, rose, red, red-violet, and white, often with bands of a lighter or darker shade. The plants are biennial, sometimes behaving as perennials.

China pinks (*Dianthus chinensis*) are usually grown as annuals. The flowers come in shades of red, pink, and white, blooming on upright plants 1 to 1½ feet tall.

Blooming time: Late spring to midsummer

Height: 6 inches to 1½ feet

Spacing: 6 to 12 inches

Light: Full sun to partial shade; some afternoon shade is helpful where summers are hot

Soil: Average fertility; light, well-drained, sandy, with neutral to slightly alkaline pH

Moisture: Some can tolerate drought; most need average moisture

Comments: Many garden pinks have a delightful, spicy-sweet clove fragrance. Position them in the front of the garden; low forms are especially pretty spilling over the edges of a path.

Plant with the crowns right at the soil surface; do not plant too deep.

Dicentra

Bleeding Heart

Dicentra eximia, Fringed Bleeding Heart

D. spectabilis, Common Bleeding Heart

Perennial

Fringed bleeding heart and its hybrids have narrow bell-shaped flowers that dangle in clusters from thin stems that rise above a loose mound of ferny leaves. Flowers may be deep pink, red, or white, depending on the variety.

Common bleeding heart has uniquely delightful heart-shaped flowers that hang from slender horizontal stems. The bushy plants have divided leaves that are not as fine in texture as those of fringed bleeding heart.

Blooming time: Fringed bleeding heart blooms all summer; common bleeding heart in mid to late spring

Height: 1 to 2 feet; common bleeding heart is a bit larger than fringed bleeding heart

Spacing: 1½ to 2 feet

Light: Partial shade; will tolerate full sun in moist soil

Soil: Moist but well-drained, loamy, with lots of organic matter. Good drainage is essential.

Moisture: Bleeding heart cannot tolerate soggy conditions.

Comments: Bleeding heart is lovely in the front of a shady garden. In a location with adequate moisture and relatively cool temperatures, the foliage of bleeding heart remains attractive all season long. Bleeding heart does not do well in warm, arid climates. The plants die back or become dishevelled (and must be cut back) in summer, leaving a gap in the garden. Planting hostas, ferns, or other plants nearby will help camouflage the empty space. Fringed bleeding heart holds up somewhat better in heat, and the foliage retains its vigor all season.

Digitalis
Foxglove
Digitalis purpurea
Biennial

Foxglove's majestic spikes of tubular flowers in shades of purple, rose, pink, and cream are carried on strong vertical stems above basal clumps of narrow, oblong leaves. Foxgloves are large plants of rather bold texture; they are not delicate.

Blooming time: Late spring or early summer

Height: 2 to 5 feet

Spacing: 1 to 2 feet

Light: Partial shade to full sun

Soil: Fertile, moist but well-drained, with lots of organic matter

Moisture: Average

Comments: Foxgloves add handsome vertical accents to the middle or back of the garden, and are classic cottage garden flowers. They are also good for cutting.

Plants usually rebloom, with somewhat smaller flower spikes, if cut back after they finish their first flowering. They may also self-sow.

Foxgloves prefer some shade, but will adapt to full sun. All parts of the plant are poisonous if eaten.

Dracaena
Dracaena indivisa
Tender perennial

The foliage plant usually sold as *Dracaena indivisa* is known to botanists as *Cordyline indivisa*. By either name, the plant boasts long, narrow, sword-shaped green leaves that come from a central point and grow upright, their tips arching gracefully in a fountain shape.

Height: 2 to 3 feet when grown as an annual

Spacing: 1 foot apart if planting more than one

Light: Full sun, partial shade, or shade

Soil: Moist but well-drained, average fertility

Moisture: Average

Comments: This narrow-leaved foliage plant is a popular source of height and vertical line in container plantings. Use it in the center of a freestanding container or in the back of a container that will be viewed from one side. The smooth leaves add a sleek, clean line that makes a good foil for the softer shapes of flowering plants.

Although usually grown as an annual, you can dig up the plant in fall, before the weather turns cold, replant it in a large, deep pot (that will accommodate the long taproot which develops), and bring it indoors as a houseplant.

Eustoma

Lisianthus
Eustoma grandiflorum
Annual

Lovely flowers shaped like wide, shallow cups, in shades of pink, lavender, rich purple, and white, forming at the tips of the stems. Plants are upright and branched, not really bushy, with oval to elongated, soft-textured leaves of a slightly grayish green.

Blooming time: Midsummer, continuing into late summer if conditions are favorable
Height: 1 to 3 feet, depending on cultivar
Spacing: About 1 foot apart
Light: Full sun to partial shade
Soil: Moist but well-drained, average to good fertility
Moisture: Even moisture; plants do not like dry soil, especially when growing in containers; they wilt easily
Comments: Lisianthus is a stunning cut flower with a charming, old-fashioned look. Plant it in the front to middle of the garden. The plants are also handsome in individual pots; try placing the pots on stairs, or massing them on top of a wall.

Lisianthus grows best in warm weather, but may fatigue during hot, humid spells. Plant out after frost danger is past in spring.

The plant is also known as prairie gentian.

Festuca

Fescue
Festuca ovina var. *glauca,* Dwarf blue fescue
Perennial

This small ornamental grass produces a tuft of upright, slender, round, almost needle-like leaves of a soft blue-green color.
Height: 9 to 12 inches
Spacing: 12 inches
Light: Full sun
Soil: Average fertility; well-drained
Moisture: Average
Comments: Dwarf blue fescue's compact size allows it a multiplicity of uses in gardens of any size. Smaller and neater than most ornamental grasses, blue fescue can edge an informal garden of relatively large plants, or you can plant it in masses as a groundcover.

Fuchsia

Fuchsia hybrids
Tender perennial grown as annual

Fuchsia's dangling flowers consist of a bell-shaped calyx under wide-spreading petals, in shades of red, purple, pink, or white; many varieties have bicolored blossoms. Plants have long, cascading stems with rather small, oval leaves.
Blooming time: All summer
Height: Stems grow roughly 1½ to 2 feet long
Spacing: If using as bedding plants, set about 1 foot apart
Light: Partial shade to shade
Soil: Moist but well-drained, average fertility
Moisture: Plants need even, regular moisture
Comments: Although shrubby in warm climates, fuchsias are ideal for hanging baskets farther north; the stems arc gracefully over the sides of the container.

In warm climates, fuchsias may be grown outdoors all year.

Gaillardia
Blanket Flower
Gaillardia ×*grandiflora,* Perennial Blanket Flower
G. pulchella, Annual Blanket Flower
Annual or perennial

Perennial gaillardia bears daisylike flowers up to 4 inches across; they have domed, red to red-purple centers, and petals (actually correctly called ray flowers) that are red tipped with golden yellow. The annual species, *Gaillardia pulchella,* has disc-shaped or ball-shaped flowers of gold, red, or red tipped with yellow. Plants are upright and branched, with lance-shaped, irregularly notched leaves of medium to deep green; the leaves may be spotted in the perennial type.

Blooming time: Mid to late summer
Height: Perennial blanket flower grows from approximately 6 inches to 3 feet, depending upon variety; annual blanket flower grows about 1 foot tall
Spacing: 9 inches to 1½ feet
Light: Full sun
Soil: Average fertility; good drainage is important. Plants will not thrive in dense, soggy soils
Moisture: Gaillardia can tolerate some drought
Comments: The cheerful flowers of gaillardia are most at home in informal gardens, because the plants tend to look a bit dishevelled and weedy by late summer. Position perennials according to their mature height, placing smaller varieties in the front of the garden and taller types in the middle or background. Perennials are also nice additions to meadow gardens. The smaller annual type belongs in the front of the garden, or in containers or windowboxes.

Blanket flowers are hardy and can go out into the garden in spring. Warm-climate gardeners can grow the annual type for winter flowers.

Gladiolus
Gladiolus cultivars
Tender corm

Gladiolus bears spikes of trumpet-shaped flowers with flared, ruffled edges, in many shades of red, rose, pink, purple, salmon, yellow and gold, also white, light green, and bicolors, on unbranched stems. The plants have stiff, sword-shaped leaves.

Blooming time: Mid to late summer, depending on cultivar and time of planting
Height: To 3 feet and more
Spacing: 3 to 6 inches, depending on mature height
Light: Full sun
Soil: Fertile, moist but well-drained
Moisture: Water regularly in dry weather
Comments: Gladiolus is easiest to grow by itself, or in the back of a cutting garden. The flowers are long-lasting when cut and placed in a big vase. They are difficult to combine with other flowers in bouquets and arrangements, and are best displayed by themselves. The plants add a smooth vertical line to the garden.

Make successive plantings until midsummer, beginning after all danger of frost is past in spring, to produce flowers for cutting over an extended period. If you live north of zone 8, dig the bulbs six weeks after flowering is over and store them indoors in a cool, dry place over winter.

Gypsophila

Baby's Breath

Gypsophila elegans, Annual Baby's Breath

G. paniculata, Perennial Baby's Breath

Annual or perennial

Clouds of little white or pink flowers cover branched, narrow-leaved plants. Although much-branched, the plants' slender, sharply angled stems and small leaves give them a light texture in the garden. The annual type has larger flowers (up to an inch across) on smaller plants than the perennial species.

Blooming time: Mid to late summer; relatively short-blooming

Height: 1 to 3 feet, depending on species and variety

Spacing: 1 to 2 feet

Light: Full sun; plants appreciate partial afternoon shade in warm climates

Soil: Fertile, well-drained, with a neutral to slightly alkaline pH

Moisture: Average

Comments: Although it does not bloom for very long, baby's breath is a wonderful filler in fresh or dried bouquets, and can perform the same function in the garden. Plants fill the space with a haze of gauzy, fluffy white confetti for the few weeks they are in flower. The plants like to spread out, and can cover holes left by poppies, spring phlox, or bulbs that bloomed earlier in the season.

If you can find young plants in a local garden center over a number of weeks you can plant the annual type in several successions two weeks apart to extend the blooming period.

Perennial baby's breath may need staking to support the stems when plants are in bloom. Make a supporting structure by placing four canes or slender stakes around the plant, and wrapping some twine or heavy string around the canes to support the branches.

Hedera

English Ivy

Hedera helix

Perennial

English ivy's glossy dark green foliage grows on long stems that will either climb or trail across the ground. There are many cultivars with different leaf shapes and sizes, and assorted variegation patterns with gold and white.

Height: 8 to 10 inches when grown as a groundcover; can also be allowed to climb a brick or stone wall

Spacing: 6 to 12 inches

Light: Partial shade, shade, or sun

Soil: Adapts to practically any soil

Moisture: Average

Comments: Ivy is durable and extremely easy to grow—a good groundcover for difficult areas. It can become invasive, however, and must be kept under control by clipping back the stems when necessary.

English ivy will eventually create a dense screen when grown as a climber. It will cling to brick or stonework with no help from the gardener.

Helianthus and Heliopsis

Sunflower

Helianthus species *Heliopsis helianthoides*

Annual or perennial

Golden daisy flowers, also in shades of orange, mahogany, maroon, and cream; some have large brown centers. One species, *Helianthus annuus,* includes the giant sunflower that provides seeds for birds and human snackers; its flowers can easily grow to 1 foot across.

Most species grow on upright, branched plants with large, coarse leaves.

Blooming time: Mid to late summer
Height: 3 to 4 feet; up to 10 or even 12 feet for the giant sunflower
Spacing: 1½ to 2 feet
Light: Full sun to partial shade
Soil: Any average garden soil
Moisture: Best with even moisture, but can tolerate dryness
Comments: These tall, golden flowers for the back of the garden are easy to grow and long-blooming. Giant sunflowers can be planted in a row, where their tall, straight stems will form a border or light screen.

Sunflowers are cheerful, lively plants that are most at home in informal gardens; they are too unrefined for most formal beds and borders. Dwarf varieties are most versatile in the garden.

Sunflowers grow best in warm weather, but are reasonably hardy when established. Plant them out when all danger of frost is past in spring.

Hemerocallis
Daylily
Hemerocallis cultivars
Perennial

The big, trumpet-shaped flowers of hybrid daylilies are now available in a host of warm colors, pastels and brights—maroon, red, red-orange, orange, apricot, pink, peach, gold, yellow, and buff, on tall, straight stems above strap-shaped leaves. The flowers of some varieties are sweetly fragrant.

Blooming time: Early to late summer, depending on variety
Height: 2 to 5 feet
Spacing: 1½ to 2 feet
Light: Full sun to partial shade; stems bend toward the light in shady places
Soil: Adapts to any reasonable soil, but grows best in moist but well-drained soil of average fertility, with lots of organic matter
Moisture: Needs no watering except during prolonged dry spells
Comments: Daylilies are easy to grow and lovely in the middle or back of the garden. Or plant them in masses for a border or divider, or along a driveway or sidewalk. Dwarf varieties such as Stella de Oro are perfect for a tub or the front of the garden.

As the name implies, individual flowers last only a single day, but each plant produces a succession of flowers over a period of two to three or more weeks. For a longer season of bloom, plant early, midseason, and late varieties.

Heuchera
Coralbells
Heuchera ×*brizoides, H.* cultivars
Perennial

Airy sprays of tiny bell-shaped flowers in shades of red, pink, or white are borne on slender stems above a low mound of rounded, ivy-shaped leaves. The variety Palace Purple has white flowers and bronzy purple leaves.

Blooming time: Late spring to midsummer
Height: 1 to 1½ feet when not in bloom; flower stems grow approximately 2 to 2½ feet tall
Spacing: 1 foot
Light: Best in partial shade, but also does well in full sun
Moisture: Average
Comments: Plant coralbells near the front or middle of the garden. The delicate, airy flowers are good for cutting. The leaves are

pretty all season, even when the plant is not in bloom.

Hibiscus
Rose Mallow
Hibiscus moscheutos
Perennial

Large, open, slightly bell-shaped flowers with prominent fused stamens in the center typify hibiscus; they bloom in shades of pink, rose, pale yellow, or white. The flowers can be 6 or more inches across. Plants have large, oval to nearly heart-shaped leaves on thick stems.

Blooming time: Mid to late summer; long-blooming

Height: 3 to 8 feet

Spacing: 3 to 6 feet

Light: Full sun

Moisture: Average

Comments: The huge, broad, cup-shaped to saucerlike flowers of hibiscus bring an exotic, tropical feeling to the garden. You can plant them in the back of the garden, as a border by themselves, as specimens or focal points in a lawn, or in large tubs (plants in tubs will remain smaller). Hibiscus is especially valuable because it blooms for much of the summer.

The plants are not hardy in cold climates (north of zone 5) but they may be grown as annuals in northern gardens. Do not set out plants until after all danger of frost is past in spring.

You may also see at the garden center a smaller, shrubbier-looking hibiscus, with woody stems and flowers in an assortment of warm shades. This species is not hardy, although it looks like it should be. Unless you live in a frost-free climate you will have to bring this type indoors as a houseplant in winter.

Hosta
Plantain Lily
Hosta species
Perennial

Hostas are grown primarily for their foliage, which comes in a range of green shades, from chartreuse to blue-green. Many cultivars are variegated in gold or white, in assorted patterns. Some leaves have a puckered, quilted texture, others are smooth. The leaves are oval to elongated, in the form of a low rosette. Bell-shaped flowers resembling small lilies in white or lavender bloom in clusters on tall stems; some are fragrant.

Blooming time: Mid to late summer

Height: Many sizes, from dwarf varieties with leaves 6 inches long, to large-leaved plants with flower stems 4 or 5 feet high above a mound of foliage 3 feet tall.

Spacing: 1 to 3 feet, depending on variety

Light: Partial shade to shade; can tolerate full sun if the soil is rich and moist

Soil: Fertile, well-drained, rich in organic matter, with a slightly acid to neutral pH

Moisture: Plants need even moisture in summer; drier conditions in winter when plants are dormant

Comments: Hostas are welcome in shady gardens, where they are effective massed in the front or middle of beds or borders, as dictated by their size. They are easy to grow and very hardy, and seldom need division.

The diversity of plant sizes and colors is impressive. You could easily plant an interesting garden of nothing but hostas, as collectors do. New cultivars are continually being developed, with variations in size, leaf color, texture, and variegation patterns.

Iberis

Candytuft
Iberis sempervirens, Perennial Candytuft
I. umbellata, Globe Candytuft
Annual or perennial

Small plants bear rounded or flat-topped clusters an inch or two across of small, dainty flowers in white or shades or pink and lavender. Perennial candytuft is a sprawling, low-growing plant with glossy leaves that are evergreen in good conditions; globe candytuft is an upright, branched annual plant with small, narrow green leaves.

Blooming time: Perennials bloom in mid to late spring; annuals from late spring to early fall

Height: Perennial candytuft grows 4 to 10 inches tall; globe candytuft to 14 inches

Spacing: 6 to 10 inches

Light: Full sun is best; plants will bloom, but be of lesser quality, in partial shade

Soil: Moist but well-drained, average to good fertility

Moisture: Water deeply during dry weather, especially perennials; the annual type can tolerate a bit of drought

Comments: The crisp white blossoms of perennial candytuft are especially lovely with spring bulbs; the plant is also pretty in a rock garden, or planted along a stone wall.

Easy to grow and charming in the front of the garden, globe candytuft is a pretty edging plant; it often self-sows and comes back the following year. Shear back plants after the first flush of bloom and they will rebloom with new vigor.

Both types of candytuft grow best in cool weather.

Impatiens

Impatiens cultivars
Tender perennial grown as annual

Flowers in every imaginable shade of pink, also red, orange, lavender, and white, some with a contrasting eye, some with full, double flowers, on bushy, rather mounded plants with oval leaves. The New Guinea hybrids, true annuals, have larger flowers, mostly in shades of red, rose, lavender, and pink, on taller plants with longer leaves that are often veined with red and shaded with yellow in the center. Some have dark red-purple leaves.

Blooming time: All summer until frost

Height: Bedding varieties grow 4 to 12 inches tall, depending on variety; New Guinea impatiens reaches 1 to 2 feet in height

Spacing: 10 to 12 inches

Light: Partial shade to shade; will also grow in sun with enough moisture. New Guinea impatiens likes more sun, and will grow in full sun to partial shade

Soil: Moist but well-drained, of average fertility, with lots of organic matter is ideal, but plants will adapt to a range of soils

Moisture: Needs even, regular moisture

Comments: Bedding impatiens is widely grown—perhaps too widely—but is still hard to beat for massing in the front of shady beds and borders, under shrubs, in pots, window-boxes, and hanging baskets. It is easy to grow and among the most versatile of garden plants.

New Guinea impatiens is a taller, flashier plant for the middle of sunny to partly shady gardens, or for containers.

Neither type of impatiens can take cold, so do not plant them out until all danger of frost is past and the weather has warmed in spring.

Impatiens does not require dead-heading—old flowers will drop off by themselves.

The double-flowered type tends to drop many of its pretty blossoms shortly after they open, so handle plants with extreme care.

Ipomoea
Morning Glory
Ipomoea species
Annual

Romantic, funnel-shaped blossoms with wide petals of sky blue, white, pink, crimson, lavender, or purple, on gracefully tendrilled, twining vines with heart-shaped green leaves.

Blooming time: Early or midsummer (depending on when plants are started) to frost

Height: 6 to 8 feet

Spacing: 6 to 9 inches

Light: Full sun

Soil: Average, well-drained; tolerates poor soil

Moisture: Best with even moisture

Comments: Morning glories are often grown from seed, but started plants are available in many garden centers; transplant them to the garden with care.

Fast-growing morning glories are ideal for quick screening, and can be trained on trellises, fences, screens, or posts. The twining vines do not need to be fastened to their supports—they will attach themselves. You could also grow morning glories in hanging baskets and let the long vines trail to the ground. They are wonderful in cottage gardens, or grown on a trellis along the side of a shed or garage.

The most popular variety, Heavenly Blue, is an ethereal true blue, a color not easily found in the plant world.

The plants grow best in warm weather, and cannot tolerate frost. True to their name, the flowers open in the morning, and close by late afternoon.

Iris
Iris cultivars, Bearded Iris
I. sibirica, Siberian Iris
Perennial

Lovely, graceful flowers composed of three upright petals and three drooping petals called "falls," with or without the tuft of hairs known as a beard. Flowers come in many shades of yellow, gold, apricot, orange, pink, magenta, maroon, brownish red, lavender, orchid, blue, blue-violet, purple, deep purple-black, and pale green, as well as white. Flowers appear on upright stems above a clump of long, sword-shaped to narrow and grassy leaves.

Blooming time: Each variety blooms for one to three weeks, but the iris season extends from late spring to early summer. You can plant early, midseason, and late varieties for extended bloom.

Height: 6 inches to 6 feet, depending on variety

Spacing: 6 inches to 3 feet, depending on variety

Light: Most need full sun, at least six hours a day; some afternoon shade is helpful in warm climates

Soil: Moist but well-drained, reasonably fertile, rich in organic matter. Bearded irises like a neutral to slightly alkaline pH; Siberians prefer neutral to slightly acid soil

Moisture: Average

Comments: Irises are lovely in the front, middle, or back of the garden, according to their mature height. Large types make a handsome border or divider all by themselves.

The irises with which we are concerned here grow from rhizomes; there are also bulbous types. Plant bearded irises so the top of the rhizome is even with the soil surface. The rhizome should not be covered with soil except in hot climates. Plant with the fan of leaves pointing in the direction you want the plants to grow. If planting a group of irises, position them so all the leaf fans point in the same direction.

Plant Siberian iris at the same depth it was growing in its nursery container.

Plants may not grow well in the extreme North or South.

When the rhizomes of bearded iris become crowded after three or four years, dig and divide them, discarding the old central parts of the rhizome clumps and replanting the younger, outer parts.

Siberian irises are easy to grow, reliable, and less work than beardeds. Divide them when the clumps become crowded.

Lantana

Yellow Sage
Lantana camara
Tender perennial

Wide, flat clusters to 2 inches across or small flowers of white, yellow, pinkish lavender; or cream changing to pink, pink to lavender, or yellow changing to orange; or a yellow, red, and brown combination, on upright, branched, bushy plants with toothed, oval leaves. The plants are shrubby in climates where they are perennial. In color-changing varieties, flower clusters may contain three colors at once.

Blooming time: All summer
Height: Plants reach 4 feet in mild climates where they are perennial; when grown as annuals they are likely to be closer to 2 feet.
Spacing: 1½ to 2½ feet

Light: Full sun
Soil: Well-drained, average fertility; tolerates poor soil
Moisture: Lantana can tolerate some dryness
Comments: An interesting plant for a large container, as well as the center or back of the garden. Children find the color-changing flowers magical.

Lantana is salt-tolerant and useful in seashore gardens. Its flowers are attractive to butterflies.

Plants grow best in warm weather. Except in warm climates, bring lantana indoors over winter or grow it as an annual.

There are also trailing varieties to grow in hanging baskets.

Lavender

Lavandula angustifolia, English lavender
Perennial

Small spikes of tiny purple flowers, lavender to deep violet, depending on variety, are carried atop slender, wandlike stems; the shrubby, sprawling plants have silvery green leaves, and stems that become woody as they age. Both flowers and leaves possess the distinctive, refreshing fragrance. There is also a white-flowered form.

Blooming time: Midsummer
Height: 1 to 3 feet, depending on variety
Spacing: 1½ to 3 feet, depending on variety and growing conditions
Light: Full sun
Soil: Light, well-drained, gravelly soil is ideal; needs a pH around neutral. Lavender will not thrive in dense, soggy soil.
Moisture: Average
Comments: Loved for its fresh, clean scent, lavender is as at home in the front of a flower garden as it is in an herb garden. It is heavenly

planted in masses, or along the edge of a path where passersby will brush against it and release the scent.

Lilium
Lily
Lilium species and cultivars
Hardy bulb

The trumpet-shaped flowers of lilies face upward, out, or down; the flowers of some varieties have reflexed petals. The extensive color range includes white, cream, many shades of yellow, gold, apricot, orange, pink, and red; some flowers are spotted, some are fragrant. The plants have tall, straight, upright stems with pairs of narrow leaves arranged along their length; the flowers appear in branched clusters.

Blooming time: Early to late summer, depending on variety
Height: 2½ to 6 feet or more
Spacing: 8 to 12 inches, depending on variety
Light: Full sun to partial shade, depending on variety. Many lilies like to have their tops in the sun and their roots in the shade.
Soil: Light, moist but well-drained, with lots of organic matter. Lilies do not tolerate soggy soil.
Moisture: When plants are in active growth, water weekly or as necessary to keep the soil moist (but not wet). Cut back on watering when plants finish blooming.
Comments: Lilies are classic summer flowers, good for cutting and appropriate for either formal or informal gardens. Put lilies in the middle or back of the garden. When planting bulbs, plant three times as deep as the height of the bulb.

Lilies appreciate a mulch that keeps their roots cool and shaded. Fertilize with an all-purpose fertilizer once or twice in spring. Stake tall varieties to support the weight of the flowers.

Lobelia
Lobelia erinus, Edging Lobelia
Annual

Little flowers of deep blue, sky blue, red, pink, or white cover compact plants with small elliptical leaves. Colored flowers often have a white eye (center).

Blooming time: All summer
Height: 4 to 6 inches
Spacing: 6 inches
Light: Full sun to partial shade; plants appreciate afternoon shade where summers are hot
Soil: Moist but well-drained, fertile, rich in organic matter
Moisture: Needs even moisture all summer, but soil must not be soggy
Comments: These small, delicate-looking plants are lovely in the front of a windowbox or container, where they will spill over the sides. Or use them as edging in a partly shaded garden. The flowers of the blue varieties positively glow in the shade.

Lobelia may stop blooming in hot, humid weather, and plants may die back. If flowering slows, cut back the plants to encourage reblooming—they often recover later in summer, when nighttime temperatures begin to cool off.

Lobularia
Sweet Alyssum
Lobularia maritima
Annual

Tiny flowers of white, lavender, pink, or purple, with a sweet honey fragrance cover low, sprawling plants with little green leaves.

Blooming time: From spring right through summer, into autumn
Height: Usually 4 to 6 inches, may grow as high as 12 inches
Spacing: 6 inches
Light: Full sun to partial shade
Soil: Well-drained, average fertility
Moisture: Average
Comments: Sweet alyssum is a low-growing, light-textured favorite for edging and tumbling over the front of containers or windowboxes. It is also quite nice rambling among the stones in a rock garden. For a different look, plant sweet alyssum in clumps or drifts among other plants in the front of the garden; it makes an appealing carpet at the feet of clematis or lilies growing near the outside of a garden bed.

Plants grow best in cool weather and can go into the garden as soon as the danger of heavy frost is past in spring. If bloom slows in midsummer and plants partially die back, shear back the plants and they will rebloom with new energy.

Sweet alyssum is easy to grow and plants may self-sow or return, although with less vigor, in subsequent years. Plan on starting with fresh plants every year.

Marjoram
Sweet Marjoram
Origanum majorana
Tender perennial grown as annual

This culinary herb is grown for its aromatic, oval, grayish green leaves; tiny white flowers in small clusters appear in summer. Marjoram is a small, bushy plant of soft texture.
Height: to 1 foot
Spacing: 6 to 8 inches
Light: Full sun

Soil: Light, well-drained, average fertility
Moisture: Plants prefer somewhat dry soil
Comments: Marjoram is invaluable in the kitchen and attractive in the front of the garden. It is also eminently well-suited to container culture. Pinch back the plants when flower buds form, to postpone bloom and maintain the neat shape of the plants.

Monarda
Beebalm
Monarda didyma
Perennial

Clusters of tubular flowers surrounded by slender bracts (modified leaves), in shades of red, pink, purple, and white, bloom atop tall, straight stems. Pairs of aromatic, oval, dark green leaves line the square stems.
Blooming time: Summer
Height: 2½ to 3 feet
Spacing: 1½ feet
Light: Full sun to partial shade
Soil: Moist, fertile
Moisture: Even moisture is best
Comments: Beebalm is noteworthy for its unusual flower clusters, and has fragrant leaves as well. An attractive plant for the middle or back of the garden, it works best in informal designs. The citrus-scented leaves can be dried and used for tea; in fact, one of its nicknames is Oswego tea. Beebalm, as its name implies, attracts bees when in bloom.

A member of the Mint Family, beebalm spreads and, like other members of the mint clan, it can become invasive. It does not do well in dry soil and may develop mildew. Plantings will need division every two or three years to maintain the vigor of the plants.

by late summer, and plants will start to die back in early autumn.

Myosotis

Forget-me-not
Myosotis scorpioides, True Forget-me-not
M. sylvatica, Annual Forget-me-not
Annual or perennial

Forget-me-not's clusters of small flowers of celestial blue, pink, or white are carried on slender stems above a mound or mat of smooth, oblong, tongue-shaped leaves.

Blooming time: The perennial true forget-me-not blooms in spring; the annual type blooms from spring into summer

Height: 6 inches to 1½ feet

Spacing: 6 to 10 inches

Light: Partial to light shade is preferred; will also grow in full sun in moist soil

Soil: Moist but well-drained, with lots of organic matter

Moisture: Plants need even, constant moisture, but not sogginess

Comments: Forget-me-nots are lovely at the edge of a woods, in a woodland garden in light shade, and as a carpet under spring bulbs. They are also pretty in a container garden with daffodils and other bulbs. You can also grow them in a rock garden.

Perennial forget-me-nots are usually short-lived, but are likely to self-sow and colonize their immediate area if they are not deadheaded.

Myosotis sylvatica (also sold as *M. alpestris*) is an annual, or a biennial grown as an annual. Like the perennial species, this type also may self-sow.

Plants grow best in cool weather, and can go into the garden when danger of heavy frost is past in spring. They are sometimes prone to mildew. The foliage may begin to turn brown

Nepeta

Catmint
Nepeta mussinii
Perennial

Loose spires of small, tubular flowers of lavender-purple, mauve, or white top bushy plants with small, oval to heart-shaped, toothed leaves of slightly grayish green. The leaves have a citrusy fragrance. Plants have a sprawling, spreading habit.

Blooming time: Early to late summer; plants bloom almost all summer if deadheaded regularly or sheared back after the first flush of bloom

Height: 1 to 1½ feet

Spacing: 1 to 2 feet

Light: Full sun to partial shade

Soil: Light, sandy, well-drained, of average fertility

Moisture: Average, but catmint can tolerate some drought

Comments: A lively, exuberant plant for the front of an informal border, catmint is especially pretty along a path, where the plants can spill into the walkway. The colors blend well with many other flowers, particularly rose, pink, blue, and yellow shades.

Like most other members of the Mint Family, nepeta spreads and can look weedy. Cut back the plants when they get out of hand; they will regrow. Where space is limited, divide plantings every few years to keep them under control.

Catmint likes hot, sunny conditions, and will grow in poor, sandy soil.

Look for cultivars of *Nepeta mussinii,* which you may find labeled (mistakenly) as *N. ×faassenii.*

Nicotiana
Flowering Tobacco
Nicotiana alata
Tender perennial grown as annual

Star-shaped white, red, rose, pink, lavender, or light green flowers with long, tubular throats bloom on branched, bushy plants with rather large, narrow to oblong leaves of medium green. The plants have an open, rather than a dense, form. They are covered with soft hairs and feel rather sticky to the touch, similar to petunias which, like nicotiana, belong to the same botanical family as tomatoes and potatoes. The flowers of the species form are fragrant at night, but most of the commonly available hybrids have only a faint scent after sundown.

Blooming time: All summer, if deadheaded regularly
Height: 1 to 3 feet; the species form grows to 5 feet
Spacing: 9 to 12 inches
Light: Full sun to partial shade
Soil: Moist but well-drained, of average fertility
Moisture: Nicotiana needs watering during spells of hot, dry weather
Comments: Easy to grow and a prolific bloomer, nicotiana is a charming plant to add mass and color in the front or middle ground of a bed or border. It flowers happily in containers, as well. Place the species form and larger hybrids in the back of the garden.

A most versatile plant, nicotiana performs well in hot sun if given enough water, and also blooms nicely in partial to light shade.

If you deadhead regularly, the plants will bloom all summer. When deadheading, cut off the old flower right below its base; new buds will develop on the stem immediately below the old blossom.

Do not set out plants until all danger of frost is past in spring. The leaves and flowers are delicate and easily damaged; handle plants carefully during transplanting. Japanese beetles love nicotiana, so take appropriate measures if these bugs are a problem in your garden.

Nierembergia
Cup Flower
Nierembergia hippomanica
Tender perennial grown as annual

This delightful little plant is showing up in more garden centers and local nurseries, and with good reason. Its small, cup-shaped flowers are up to an inch wide; they are white to pale blue or, in one cultivar, violet, with yellow inside the throat. The flowers practically cover the delicate, thin-stemmed, bushy plants, which have narrow, almost needlelike leaves. Cup flower is a fine-textured plant whose thin stems and small leaves give it an open, airy look.

Blooming time: Summer
Height: 6 to 14 inches
Spacing: 8 to 10 inches
Light: Full sun to partial shade
Soil: Moist but well-drained, average fertility
Moisture: Average
Comments: Grow the dainty cup flower in the front of a garden of small plants or in containers, where it can be seen close-up and

appreciated. It is a perfect windowbox plant; its slender stems will droop gracefully over the edge. Don't let nierembergia dry out too much between waterings; it likes regular moisture.

Oregano

Origanum heracleoticum, Greek oregano
Perennial

Aromatic, flavorful, widely oval leaves to 2 inches long grace branched, bushy plants.
Blooming time: Oregano is grown for its leaves, but bears small, edible white flowers in summer
Height: 1 to 2 feet
Spacing: 6 to 8 inches
Light: Full sun
Soil: Light, well-drained, of average fertility
Moisture: Best when kept a little on the dry side
Comments: The species recommended here, Greek oregano, is the most flavorful kind of oregano. You may also find it listed as *Origanum vulgare* subsp. *hirtum.* To make sure you are getting the real thing, and not inferior wild marjoram, brush a leaf with your finger—it should release the characteristic scent.

Plant oregano in the front or middle of a sunny garden, or grow it in pots on a deck or patio.

Pachysandra

Pachysandra terminalis
Perennial

A classic groundcover grown for its whorls of glossy, deep green, lobed leaves; there is also a cultivar variegated with white. Plants may be evergreen in good conditions. The foliage forms low mats.
Blooming time: Small white flowers in spring are not really noteworthy
Height: 4 to 6 inches
Spacing: 8 to 12 inches
Light: Partial to deep shade; does not grow well in sun
Soil: Moist, loose, with lots of organic matter, of average fertility; but pachysandra will adapt to a range of soils from stony to clay
Moisture: Cannot stand drought; needs watering in dry weather
Comments: One of the most widely grown and still one of the best groundcovers for shady areas. Plants spread quickly, and if trimming is needed to keep them in bounds, the trimmings can be rooted and replanted somewhere else.

Pachysandra is especially attractive under trees and in shady gardens with bulbs and perennials.

Paeonia

Peony
Paeonia lactiflora, P. officinalis
Perennial

Large single or full, double flowers in white, cream, many shades of pink, rose, and red, also peach and yellow, often sweetly fragrant. Some varieties have fewer petals and large, golden centers. The divided leaves are handsome all season. Although they die back to the ground each winter, peonies have the form of a small bush during the growing season.
Blooming time: Late spring
Height: To about 3 feet
Spacing: 3 feet
Light: Full sun to partial shade
Soil: Moist but well-drained, with lots of organic matter, of average to high fertility. Good drainage is important

Moisture: Average

Comments: Peonies are easy to grow, long-lived, and need little maintenance. Plant them individually in beds and borders with perennials, or in a row as a border or divider. The lovely flowers are excellent for cutting.

Plants appreciate afternoon shade where summers are quite hot.

If planted too deep, peonies will not bloom. Plant with the crowns (the point where roots meet stem) no more than 2 inches below the soil surface.

The flowers may attract ants, but will not be harmed by them. Check flowers cut to bring indoors and shake off any ants before bringing the flowers inside.

Papaver

Poppy

Papaver nudicaule, Iceland Poppy

P. orientale, Oriental Poppy

Perennial

Poppies bear glorious, large, open flowers with fluted, ruffled petals in shades of yellow, orange, salmon, pink, red, and white. Oriental poppies are larger, with contrasting dark centers. Both types produce their flowers one at a time on tall stems above a low mound of leaves. The leaves and stems of both types are covered with hairs, which can be prickly and irritating on oriental poppies.

Blooming time: Late spring to early summer; Iceland poppies may continue blooming well into summer

Height: Iceland poppies produce smaller flowers on smaller plants, growing 1 to 2 feet high; oriental poppies reach 3 to 4 feet

Spacing: 1 to 2 feet

Light: Full sun preferred; light shade is acceptable

Soil: Light sandy or loamy soil with excellent drainage is what poppies need. Average fertility is fine for Iceland poppies; orientals need somewhat richer soil

Moisture: Average

Comments: Poppy plants may take a few years to establish themselves in the garden and reach their peak beauty, but they are worth the wait. The long-stemmed flowers are lovely for cutting, and belong in the front or middle of the garden, according to height. Oriental poppies may need staking.

Oriental poppies are very hardy, and in fact do not grow well in warm climates. The plants go dormant after blooming; planting wide-spreading summer bloomers such as baby's breath and nepeta next to them will help fill the gap left by the dormant poppies.

Iceland poppies are more difficult to grow, and are often grown as annuals. In warm climates they make good winter flowers.

Poppies do not transplant well, so handle them with care during transplanting, retaining as much of the original soil ball as possible to minimize root disturbance. Both types grow best in cool weather.

Parsley

Petroselinum crispum

Biennial

The deep green leaves are flat and divided in Italian parsley, tightly frilled in curly parsley. The leaves grow in a clump, and plants bloom their second year.

Height: Curly parsley grows 8 to 12 inches high; Italian parsley grows to 1½ feet

Spacing: 6 to 8 inches

Light: Full sun to partial shade

Soil: Moist but well-drained, fertile, containing lots of organic matter

Moisture: Average

Comments: Parsley is usually grown as an annual; when plants bloom in their second year, leaf quality declines.

Curly parsley makes an interesting edging for garden beds, forming neat mounds of vibrant emerald green. Both types are also easily grown in containers.

Set out plants when the danger of heavy frost is past in spring; they can tolerate some light frost and cool temperatures.

Pelargonium

Bedding Geranium

Pelargonium ×hortorum, Zonal Geranium

P. peltatum, Ivy Geranium

Tender perennial grown as annual

These endlessly popular plants have small flowers in shades of red, rose, pink, salmon, and lavender, also white, some bicolored, gathered into round heads on zonal geraniums. Ivy-leaved geraniums bear their flowers, white or various shades of pink, in looser clusters. Leaves are rounded and scalloped on zonals, divided into pointed segments, rather like ivy leaves, on ivy geraniums. The plants are branched and bushy; zonal geraniums are upright, while ivy geraniums have a spreading, trailing habit. Zonal geraniums have sturdy, almost succulent stems; ivy geraniums have smaller leaves on thinner stems, and a more refined overall texture.

Blooming time: All summer until frost

Height: 1 to 2 feet; ivy geraniums have trailing stems to 3 feet long

Spacing: 1 to 1½ feet

Light: Full sun for zonals; ivy geraniums are at home in full sun or partial shade

Soil: Well-drained, of average fertility, not too rich in nitrogen

Moisture: Zonal types can tolerate some dryness; ivy-leaved geraniums need regular, even moisture

Comments: Zonal geraniums, so-called because of the dark bands on their scalloped leaves, can be grown in beds, and are durable plants for pots and tubs and the back of windowboxes. Not all varieties have banded leaves. Ivy-leaved geraniums work best in hanging baskets, where their stems will cascade gracefully.

Both types need regular deadheading to remove faded flowers and keep the plants blooming happily.

Geraniums are warm-weather plants, but their leaves may burn in intensely hot, humid weather. Do not plant them outdoors until all danger of frost is past and the weather has warmed in spring.

Petunia

Petunia ×hybrida

Annual

Petunias offer wide-petaled, funnel-shaped flowers in many shades of red, rose, pink, purple, also lavender-blue, yellow, and white, including bicolors striped or edged or ruffled with white. Varieties are available with frilled, ruffled, wavy and doubled flowers, and there are some cascading varieties bred for growing in hanging baskets and windowboxes. The low, bushy, branched plants have oval leaves that are substantially smaller than the flowers. Plants feel softly hairy and sticky to the touch.

Blooming time: All summer if deadheaded regularly

Height: 10 to 15 inches

Spacing: 8 to 10 inches

Light: Full sun

Soil: Any average garden soil, moist but well-drained

Moisture: Once established, petunias can tolerate dry conditions. Water only if necessary during prolonged dry spells

Comments: Grandiflora petunias have the biggest, flashiest flowers. Multiflora types bloom more heavily, with smaller, usually single flowers that are especially nice in combination with other flowers in beds and borders. Multifloras generally hold up better in heavy rain than the large grandifloras, and are more resistant to disease.

Plant all petunias near the front of the garden, or grow them in containers.

The plants are tender, so do not plant them in the garden until all danger of frost is past and the weather is warm.

If blooming slows after a couple of months, cut back the plants to give them a fresh start.

Phlox

Phlox drummondii, Annual Phlox
P. paniculata, Garden Phlox, Summer Phlox
P. subulata, Moss Pinks, Mountain Pinks
Annual or perennial

Annual phlox has clusters of red, rose, pink, lavender, purple, yellow, or white flowers at the tops of the stems, and lance-shaped leaves. Small, fragrant, disc-shaped flowers are clustered in dense pyramidal heads on garden phlox, in shades of pink, red, rose, lavender, purple, and salmon, also white. Both annual and garden phlox are upright, branched, rather bushy plants. Small pink, rose, lavender, or white flowers cover dense, low mats of needle-like leaves on moss pinks.

Blooming time: Annual phlox blooms all summer; perennial garden phlox from midsummer to frost; moss pinks in spring

Height: Annual phlox grows 8 to 18 inches high; garden phlox grows 2 to 4 feet; moss pinks to 6 inches

Spacing: Annual phlox about 10 inches apart; garden phlox 1½ to 2 feet; moss pinks about 1 foot

Light: Full sun; moss pinks grow in full sun to partial shade

Soil: Annual phlox prefers light, very well-drained, sandy loam that is reasonably fertile and has a pH near neutral; garden phlox likes fertile, humusy soil that is moist but well-drained; moss pinks thrive in well-drained soil of average fertility

Moisture: Average

Comments: Dwarf varieties of annual phlox are pretty as edging for beds and borders, or planted in pots and windowboxes. Grow the taller varieties in the front of the garden. Annual phlox is a good companion for ageratum, sweet alyssum, or China asters, and petunias in light pink and lavender shades. The flowers of some hybrids are nearly star-shaped, and some have a contrasting eye. This type of phlox grows best in cool weather, but holds up reasonably well in hot, sunny weather.

The taller perennial garden phlox is a handsome middle-of-the-border plant, and a lovely cut flower. It is prone to mildew, however, so do not crowd the plants—allow for plenty of air circulation.

Moss pinks are a groundcover plant, nice as a spring-blooming carpet on a sunny slope.

Platycodon

Balloon Flower
Platycodon grandiflorus
Perennial

The interesting buds of balloon flower really do resemble miniature balloons, then open into star-shaped flowers of blue-violet, pink, or white. The erect plants have a clump of straight stems and relatively small, toothed, oval leaves.

Blooming time: Early to late summer
Height: 1½ to 2 feet
Spacing: 1 to 1½ feet
Light: Full sun to partial shade
Soil: Light, well-drained, moderately fertile
Comments: Plant balloon flower in the front or middle of the garden. It is easy to grow and has a long blooming period. The flowers are good for cutting.

Balloon flower does not do well in hot, humid climates.

Portulaca
Rose Moss
Portulaca grandiflora
Annual

Silky, ruffly diaphanous blossoms, single or double, in many warm shades—red, rose, magenta, pink, salmon, gold, yellow, and white—grow on low, creeping plants with fleshy, needlelike foliage.

Blooming time: All summer
Height: The trailing stems grow to 10 inches long, but plants are usually no more than 6 inches tall
Spacing: 10 to 12 inches
Light: Full sun is a must
Soil: Any well-drained soil, preferably sandy; tolerates poor, dry soil
Moisture: Drought-tolerant
Comments: Portulaca is an excellent small plant for hot, dry conditions. The brilliantly colored flowers are a cheerful edging along paths and pavements, and in the front of sunny beds and borders. It is also a terrific plant for containers and hanging baskets. Some newer hybrids especially well-suited to hanging

baskets have smaller flowers and spoon-shaped leaves streaked with white and green.

Try planting portulaca in pockets of soil in stone walls, or in front of or along the top of a wall, to add a bright, festive touch. You can also use portulaca to carpet an area of poor soil.

Do not plant rose moss outdoors until all danger of frost is past in spring. The plants may self-sow; dig up unwanted volunteers and transplant them to a different spot.

Portulaca blossoms close late in the day and reopen in the morning.

Rosemary
Rosmarinus officinalis
Perennial

This small shrub is grown primarily for its flavorful, piney-scented, narrow, deep green leaves, but sufficiently mature plants also bear small blue flowers in winter or early spring with enough light.

Height: 5 to 6 feet when grown in a large container and moved outdoors in summer, or when grown outdoors in mild climates
Spacing: 1 to 3 feet
Light: Full sun
Soil: Sandy and well-drained, on the dry side, moderately fertile, mildly alkaline
Moisture: Average
Comments: Rosemary responds well to clipping and shaping, and is a good plant for formal gardens. Many growers like to train it as a topiary.

The plants grow slowly and will take years to reach a height of several feet. Rosemary cannot tolerate winter temperatures below 10 degrees Fahrenheit; in the North, grow it in a pot or tub and bring it indoors to a bright location over winter.

Rudbeckia
Coneflower
Rudbeckia fulgida, Orange Coneflower
R. hirta, Black-eyed Susan, Gloriosa Daisy
Perennial

Bright golden yellow daisy flowers with dark centers typify black-eyed Susan; the cultivar Gloriosa Daisy is flushed with red around the center. The branched plants have lance-shaped to oval leaves. *Rudbeckia hirta* and its cultivars are short-lived and are usually grown as annuals.

Blooming time: Midsummer to early autumn
Height: 2 to 3 feet
Spacing: 1 to 2 feet
Light: Full sun is best, but will tolerate some light shade
Soil: Moist but well-drained, of average fertility; will tolerate dry soil
Moisture: Average
Comments: The strident, somewhat orangey gold color is not to everyone's liking, but rudbeckia is a good, dependable plant for a meadow garden or the middle ground of an informal cutting garden.

Easy to grow and durable, the plants will tolerate hot weather and some cold, as well. *Rudbeckia fulgida* will spread, especially in light, moist soil, and needs division about every three or four years.

Salvia
Salvia farinacea, Mealycup Sage
S. splendens, Scarlet Sage
Annual or perennial

Spikes of tiny, tubular flowers on straight, slender stems, rich violet-blue in the perennial *Salvia farinacea* 'Victoria'. Cultivars of the annual *S. splendens* have smaller spikes of somewhat larger tubular blossoms of brilliant scarlet, or purple, pink, or creamy white. The upright, branched to bushy plants have oval to lance-shaped leaves.

Blooming time: All summer to frost
Height: 10 inches to 2½ feet, depending on variety
Spacing: 1 to 1½ feet. Do not crowd the plants; they become bushier as they grow
Light: Full sun; provide some afternoon shade in hot climates
Soil: Well-drained, of average fertility
Moisture: Plants need to be watered regularly in dry weather, and do not grow well in arid climates. *Salvia farinacea* is more tolerant of drought than scarlet sage.
Comments: The salvias are easy to grow and rewarding, sending up new flower spikes all summer long and needing deadheading less frequently than many other flowers. The plants provide a welcome vertical accent in the front or middle of beds and borders, or in containers.

Mealycup sage cannot tolerate cold winters, and is grown as an annual except in mild climates. Its flowers are good for cutting, and dry to a lovely soft shade of blue. There is also a white-flowered form. Victoria is an especially wonderful cultivar; it blooms all summer long and needs only occasional deadheading. If you want a hardy perennial blue salvia, look for cultivars of *Salvia ×superba,* which are often available in local outlets.

The bright red of scarlet sage can be difficult to combine with other flowers, but surrounding it with white flowers and deep green foliage makes for a very effective display. The newer, softer pink and purple shades are easier to work with.

Salvias need warm weather; do not plant them outdoors until all danger of frost is past in spring.

Sanvitalia

Creeping Zinnia
Sanvitalia procumbens
Annual

Small yellow daisy flowers with large, deep purple-brown centers, on trailing stems with small, oval leaves. The flowers actually resemble tiny sunflowers more than zinnias.

Blooming time: Summer
Height: to 6 inches
Spacing: 12 to 14 inches
Light: Full sun
Soil: Light, loose, well-drained, of average fertility
Comments: A charming, easy-to-grow little plant to use as edging or groundcover for beds and borders, or to put in the front of containers. Sanvitalia is especially nice in a hanging basket, where the stems can dangle over the sides.

The plants grow best in warm weather, so do not plant them out until the danger of frost is past in spring. Creeping zinnia holds up well in hot and humid conditions.

Sedum

Stonecrop
Sedum 'Autumn Joy'
Perennial

Autumn Joy sedum produces tight, flat heads of flowers that start out light green in late summer, change to pink, then rosy red, deepening to a beautiful coppery bronze that is difficult to describe; finally the flowers darken to a deep rust. The upright plants have fleshy leaves with scalloped edges all along the stems.

Blooming time: Late summer into fall
Height: 1½ to 2 feet
Spacing: 15 to 18 inches
Light: Full sun to partial shade
Soil: Well-drained, especially in winter when plants are dormant; of average fertility. Plants will tolerate moist soil in summer as long as it is not soggy
Moisture: Best if kept on the dry side
Comments: This cultivar is an outstanding garden plant—easy to grow and hard to beat for late-season color in the front to middle of the garden. The changing colors provide a long-lasting display, and you can leave the flower heads on the plants all winter, if you wish—they are interesting even when dry and brown.

Autumn Joy sedum is a welcome addition to an autumn garden of chrysanthemums and asters.

Senecio

Dusty Miller
Senecio cineraria
Tender perennial grown as annual

These upright, branched, bushy plants are grown for their velvety, deeply cut, silver-white foliage. The plant has a lacy, frilly look.

Height: 9 to 24 inches, depending on variety
Spacing: 10 to 12 inches
Light: Full sun
Soil: Very well-drained, of average fertility
Moisture: Average to rather dry
Comments: The silver-leaved dusty millers are valuable accents for flower gardens and containers, especially pretty with pink and blue flowers. The cool foliage can also be used to tone down plantings of hot-colored flowers, or to add shimmer to a garden of white flowers.

The plants are actually tender perennials and may winter over in warm climates. They may send up clusters of small, not very ornamental ivory or yellow flowers at the tips of upright stems; pinch out the flower stems if they appear.

Stachys
Lamb's Ears
Stachys byzantina
Perennial

Lamb's ears is grown primarily for its oval, softly fuzzy green leaves covered with silver hairs, but some gardeners also enjoy the small purple flowers that are produced on tall, rather thick stems. The plants have a sprawling, spreading habit.

Blooming time: Midsummer
Height: Leaves grow to about 1 foot; flower stems 1½ to 2 feet
Spacing: 1 foot
Light: Full sun to partial shade
Soil: Good drainage is essential; of average fertility
Moisture: Leaves will rot if the soil is too wet, but plants need water in dry weather
Comments: Lamb's ears is attractive in the front of beds and borders; if you want to let the flowers develop, plant a little farther back. The silver-white foliage beautifully complements pink, blue, and purple flowers.

Tagetes
Marigold
Tagetes erecta, African or American Marigold
T. patula, French Marigold
Annual

Marigolds bear single or fully round double flowers of yellow, orange, mahogany-red, or creamy white, on upright, bushy plants with divided, ferny foliage of deep green. The flowers of African marigolds may be 5 or 6 inches across; French marigold blossoms are usually 2 to 3 inches across.

Blooming time: From early to midsummer (depending on when plants were started) until frost
Height: American or African marigolds, 1½ to 2½ feet; French marigolds (sometimes referred to as dwarfs), 7 to 12 inches
Spacing: African marigolds, 12 to 22 inches; French marigolds, 6 to 12 inches
Light: Full sun. In hot climates plants perform better if given some afternoon shade in the height of summer
Soil: Well-drained, of average fertility
Moisture: Average
Comments: Versatile, durable, and easy to grow, marigolds thrive in hot weather and will keep blooming right up until frost if you deadhead them regularly.

The little French marigolds are perfect for windowboxes and small containers, or the front of a bed or border. Many gardeners like to edge their vegetable beds with French marigolds.

The larger-flowered types look best in the middle ground of the garden, and make good cut flowers.

Marigolds dislike cold; do not plant them out until all danger of frost is past in spring. The leaves have a pronounced scent that some gardeners enjoy and others find unpleasant.

Thunbergia
Black-eyed Susan Vine
Thunbergia alata
Tender perennial grown as annual

This vining plant bears flat, saucer-shaped, five-petaled flowers with dark brown centers and tubular throats. The flowers come in shades of orange, yellow, and creamy white, all on the same plant, and have square-edged petals. The trailing or climbing stems have triangular or arrow-shaped leaves that are coarser in texture than the smooth flowers.

Blooming time: Early to late summer
Height: Stems can grow 6 feet long
Spacing: 1 foot
Light: Full sun
Soil: Moist but well-drained, of average to good fertility
Moisture: Plants like even moisture, but don't keep them soggy
Comments: Black-eyed Susan vine can be found in many garden centers growing in a hanging basket or a pot with a small trellis. It is engaging when trained around a doorway or sunny porch, or you can grow it on a trellis or in a hanging basket.

Thunbergia is tender, so do not plant it outdoors until after all danger of frost is past and the soil has warmed in spring. The plant grows best in warm weather.

Thunbergia is also known as clock vine.

Thyme

Thymus species
Perennial

Culinary thyme is grown primarily for its small, aromatic, grayish green leaves, but produces small clusters of tiny white, pink, or lilac flowers, which are also edible. Plants are low and mat-forming, with slender vertical stems arising from horizontal stems that creep along the ground.

Blooming time: Summer
Height: 6 to 12 inches; creeping thyme grows just 2 inches high
Spacing: 6 to 10 inches
Light: Full sun
Soil: Light, loose, well-drained, of average fertility
Moisture: Good drainage is essential; thyme does not do well in wet soil
Comments: The thymes are creeping plants that will spread and can be used to carpet sunny areas of the garden. They are attractive planted between paving stones, in pockets in dry stone walls, and in the front of the garden. They also grow well in containers.

The common culinary thyme (*Thymus vulgaris*) is the most widely available kind, but you may also find tiny-leaved creeping thyme (*T. serpyllum*), or lemon-scented, golden-variegated lemon thyme (*T. citriodorus*) in a local garden center.

Thyme is easy to grow and, as a native of the Mediterranean area, very tolerant of hot, dry conditions.

Torenia

Wishbone Flower
Torenia fournieri
Annual

Enchanting tubular flowers of two shades of violet-blue and purple, or violet and white, with a yellow splash in the throat; the petals are velvety like those of pansies. The small, upright, bushy plants have more or less oval leaves. There are also varieties with white or rosy to clear pink flowers.

Blooming time: Midsummer to frost
Height: 10 to 12 inches
Spacing: 6 to 10 inches
Light: Partial shade to shade
Soil: Moist but well-drained, of average to good fertility. Torenia does not like dry soil
Moisture: Keep evenly moist, but not soggy

Top Left

*B*rowallia offers violetlike blooms on compact plants that are ideal for pots or windowboxes in partial shade.

Top Right

*T*he flowers of ageratum look like fluffy little powder puffs.

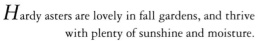

*H*ardy asters are lovely in fall gardens, and thrive with plenty of sunshine and moisture.

*T*he flowers of *Celosia cristata* come in an assortment of bizarre curled, crested, and twisted shapes.

*T*he remarkable flowers of cleome bloom atop stems that can grow to 6 feet tall in a single season.

*C*hrysanthemums are classics for autumn gardens.

Small dianthus make an engaging edging, and some are spicily fragrant.

Foxglove bears tubular flowers on tall, straight stems.

Coreopsis 'Moonbeam' is a softer shade of yellow than most other coreopsis, and with blue or pink flowers creates an especially beautiful harmony.

*D*aylilies are among the most versatile, easy-to-grow perennials. Their trumpet-shaped blossoms come in many warm colors.

*M*orning glory is an annual vine that needs warm weather in order to grow well.

*L*antana's tiny flowers are gathered into round clusters at the tips of the stems.

*S*ome varieties of impatiens have a deeper or contrasting "eye" in the center of the flower.

*P*etunias are charming in either pots or gardens. The flowers may be a solid color, striped or edged with white, or flushed or veined with a deeper color.

Rudbeckia hirta 'Gloriosa Daisy' has a red flush around the central disc.

*T*he classic black-eyed Susan form of rudbeckia looks best in informal beds and borders or in prairie and meadow gardens.

The blazing red blossoms of scarlet salvia are show-stoppers, but they are difficult to combine effectively with other flowers in the garden.

Ruffly, silky portulaca blossoms come in a host of warm colors, from pale yellow and salmon to gem-hued reds and oranges to vivid magenta.

Blue salvia is extremely versatile in the garden and adds vertical line.

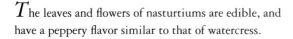

*T*he leaves and flowers of nasturtiums are edible, and have a peppery flavor similar to that of watercress.

*V*eronica flowers are carried in gracefully tapered spires that may curve at the tips. The plants sometimes have a tendency to lean toward the ground instead of standing up straight.

*F*rench marigolds are pretty in containers or as edging for small beds and borders.

Comments: These pretty little plants deserve to be better known. They are lovely for edging shady beds and borders, or massing on a shady slope or under a tree with an open, high canopy. Wishbone flower also grows well in pots and hanging baskets in partly shaded locations. It makes a nice change from or companion to impatiens.

Do not plant torenia out until all danger of frost is past in spring.

The flower gets its name from a small structure inside the throat that rather resembles a wishbone.

Tropaeolum

Nasturtium
Tropaeolum majus, T. minus
Annual

Wide-petaled, funnel-shaped, gently fragrant flowers with spurs, in shades of red, orange, pink, mahogany, yellow, and white, bloom above mounds of round, flat leaves. In newer varieties the flowers are carried above the foliage. There is also a variety with green and white variegated leaves.

Blooming time: All summer
Height: Dwarf types (*Tropaeolum minus*) grow 6 to 12 inches tall; climbing varieties (*T. majus*) can grow to 10 feet long, trailing along the ground if not fastened to a support
Spacing: 1 foot for dwarfs or climbers trained on a trellis; 2 feet for climbers allowed to sprawl on the ground
Light: Full sun to partial shade
Soil: Well-drained, of average fertility. Rich soil or too much shade will cause plants to produce lots of leaves but few flowers
Moisture: Nasturtiums can tolerate some drought

Comments: Nasturtiums are easy to grow when established, but they do not transplant terribly well, so handle with care during transplanting.

Climbing types can be attached to a trellis or screen for support, or allowed to trail from hanging baskets; or you can let them ramble about in the front of the garden. Plant dwarf types as edging, in the front of the garden, or in pots.

Nasturtiums grow best in cool weather. Warm-climate gardeners can grow them as winter flowers.

Both the lightly fragrant flowers and the leaves are edible, with a peppery flavor similar to watercress.

Verbena

Garden Verbena
Verbena ×hybrida
Annual

Verbena's round clusters of small flowers in shades of pink, rose, red, lavender, purple, yellow, and white are carried at the tips of the stems on upright or spreading plants with small, toothed or deeply divided green leaves.

Blooming time: All summer
Height: 6 to 12 inches
Spacing: 10 to 12 inches
Light: Full sun is best, but plants will bloom with a bit of light shade; in hot climates provide shade in the afternoon
Soil: Well-drained, of average fertility; verbena will adapt to sandy and poor soils
Moisture: Average
Comments: There are two types of verbena usually seen in garden centers. One type is a small, branched plant which retains an

upright form all season; this type tends to develop mildew during spells of humid, hot weather. The other type, which can be harder to find, has a more sprawling habit, with some stems shooting off in a nearly horizontal direction. Recognize this type by its leaves—they are finely cut and darker green than the leaves of the other type. This kind of verbena holds up better throughout the summer, and adds a more whimsical, fanciful look to mixed container plantings. But both verbenas are delightful in windowboxes and containers, or as edging in beds and borders.

Plants grow best in warm weather; set them out after danger of frost is past in spring.

Veronica
Speedwell
Veronica species
Perennial

Graceful, slender, tapered spikes of little violet-blue, pink, red, or white flowers on upright plants with lance-shaped leaves.

Blooming time: Early to midsummer, depending on variety
Height: 6 inches to 3 feet, depending on variety
Spacing: 1 to 1½ feet
Light: Full sun
Soil: Moist but well-drained, neither soggy nor dry; average fertility
Moisture: Average
Comments: Veronicas are lovely in the middle of beds and borders; low-growing types are nice in rock gardens and the front of the garden.

The plants tolerate heat, and their clumps of emerald green foliage are attractive even when the plants are not in bloom.

The most widely grown veronicas are violet to blue; for a change of pace try Red Fox, which has flowers of deep rose-pink.

The plants will rebloom into fall if deadheaded regularly.

Vinca
Periwinkle
Vinca minor
Perennial

Five-petaled violet-blue or white flowers bloom on trailing plants with small, oval, glossy green leaves on thin, wiry stems; there is also a form with variegated leaves.

Blooming time: Mid to late spring
Height: Plants are prostrate, creeping across the ground
Spacing: 6 to 12 inches
Light: Best in partial shade or shade, but will tolerate full sun
Soil: Well-drained, of average fertility; plants will tolerate a range of soil conditions
Moisture: Average
Comments: A widely planted and still lovely groundcover, especially useful on shady banks and in other shady places. A pretty carpet for bulbs and spring perennials. Best of all, vinca is extremely easy to grow.

Variegated vinca (*Vinca major* 'Variegata') is often grown as an annual foliage plant to trail over the edges of windowboxes and hanging baskets. You may find it labelled as "vinca vine" in garden centers.

A related tender plant grown as an annual, *Catharanthus roseus,* Madagascar periwinkle, which is often sold as vinca, has flowers in shades of pink, rose, and red, as well as white, blooms in summer, and needs full sun.

Many gardeners know *Vinca minor* by the name of myrtle.

Viola

Viola ×wittrockiana, Pansy
V. tricolor, Johnny Jump-up
Perennial grown as hardy annual

Pansies come in many shades of purple, blue, red, pink, yellow, orange, and white, with or without the distinctive clown-face markings. Johnny jump-ups are smaller, and found mostly in blue and purple shades marked with white and yellow. The plants have small oval leaves with toothed or scalloped edges, and sprawling stems that elongate as the season progresses.

Blooming time: Spring into midsummer, depending on weather conditions
Height: 6 to 10 inches for pansies; Johnny jump-ups to 12 inches
Spacing: 5 to 8 inches
Light: Full sun to partial shade
Soil: Moist, fertile, with lots of organic matter
Moisture: Plants need even, constant moisture
Comments: Pansies grow best in cool weather, and are bright and cheerful in windowboxes, pots, and as edging in springtime gardens. Regular deadheading and even moisture will keep them blooming into summer, but eventually they will succumb to the heat or become weedy and long-stemmed. When they quit, pull them up and replace them with begonias or other summer bloomers.

Johnny jump-ups are weedier looking but very appealing; they often self-sow and come back the following year.

The closely related sweet violet (*Viola odorata*) makes a good groundcover for shady places. It has small purple, blue, or white flowers in spring, and deep green, heart-shaped leaves.

Yucca

Yucca filamentosa, Adam's Needle
Perennial

Yucca's rosette of stiff, sword-shaped leaves of medium green looks like it belongs in a desert, but this species is hardy through all but the northern United States (above zone 5). In summer the plants send up branched clusters of creamy white bell-shaped flowers atop a thick stem that is 4 to 5 feet or taller. Yucca is a bold-textured, sculptural plant that works well in contemporary settings.

Blooming time: Midsummer
Height: Leaves to about 3 feet; flower stalk to 5 feet or more
Spacing: 2 to 3 feet
Light: Full sun
Soil: Light, moist but well-drained, sandy, of average fertility
Moisture: Average, but can tolerate some drought
Comments: An interesting plant for the middle or back of the garden, yucca works best in combination with other bold-leaved plants, or grown by itself. You might perhaps enjoy a planting of yucca to border a driveway.

Easy to grow and undemanding, the greatest drawback to yucca is its habit of producing vigorous suckers; these baby plants are difficult to get rid of, and give plantings of yucca a wandering habit.

Zinnia

Zinnia elegans
Annual

This flower garden favorite bears single or many-petaled double, disc-shaped flowers in pastel to bright shades of pink, rose, red, orange, gold, yellow, also white and light green, on stout-stemmed, upright, branched, rather coarse-leaved plants. Zinnias add both color and mass to the garden.

Blooming time: Midsummer to fall

Height: 6 inches to 3 feet or more, depending on variety

Spacing: 6 to 12 inches, depending on variety

Light: Full sun

Soil: Moist but well-drained, of average fertility, with lots of organic matter

Moisture: Water zinnias during dry weather; when growing in pots they need regular, abundant moisture

Comments: Zinnias are easy to grow and versatile in the garden. Their warm colors are lively and uplifting in the garden. Their folksy, informal look is ideal for a cottage garden. Use dwarfs as edging or in containers; larger varieties in the middle of the garden. The tall varieties are good for cutting.

Zinnias are prone to mildew, so don't crowd them—make sure they get plenty of air circulation. Plants grow best in warm weather.

If they have enough moisture, zinnias will hold up well in hot, intensely sunny conditions.

Appendix
Plants for Every Purpose

Easiest Plants to Grow

These plants are among the easiest to grow. They are adaptable, durable, and practically fool-proof—good choices for beginning gardeners.

Achillea

Artemisia

Aster

Brunnera, Siberian bugloss

Calendula

Chives

Coreopsis

Hedera, English ivy

Helianthus, sunflower

Heliopsis, sunflower

Hemerocallis, daylily

Hosta

Iberis, globe candytuft

Impatiens

Iris, Siberian iris

Lobularia, sweet alyssum

Nepeta, catmint

Nicotiana

Pachysandra

Paeonia, peony

Pelargonium, bedding geranium

Rudbeckia, black-eyed Susan

Salvia, mealycup or scarlet sage

Sedum

Tagetes, marigold

Vinca, periwinkle

Low-Maintenance Plants

Once established, these plants require little time to maintain.

Achillea

Ageratum

Artemisia

Astilbe

Brunnera, Siberian bugloss

Celosia

Chives

Cosmos

Dicentra, bleeding heart

Ferns

Festuca, dwarf blue fescue

Helianthus, sunflower

Heliopsis, sunflower

Hemerocallis, daylily

Hosta

Impatiens

Iris, Siberian iris

Lavender

Monarda, beebalm

Nepeta, catmint

Oregano

Paeonia, peony

Parsley

Petunia

Platycodon, balloon flower

Portulaca, rose moss

Rudbeckia, black-eyed Susan

Salvia

Sedum

Senecio, dusty miller, daylily

Tagetes, marigold

Thyme

Veronica

Vinca, periwinkle

Zinnia

Plants for Edging and Front of Garden

Ageratum

Antirrhinum, dwarf snapdragon

Artemisia, low-growing types

Begonia

Brachycome, Swan River daisy

Browallia

Brunnera, Siberian bugloss

Callistephus, China aster

Celosia, small varieties

Chives

Chrysanthemum, dwarf varieties, marguerite

Coleus

Coreopsis, smallest varieties

Dianthus, garden pinks

Eustoma, lisianthus

Festuca, dwarf blue fescue

Fuchsia

Gaillardia pulchella

Hemerocallis, dwarf daylily

Hosta, small varieties

Iberis, candytuft

Impatiens

Lavender

Lobelia, edging lobelia

Lobularia, sweet alyssum

Marjoram

Myosotis, forget-me-not

Nierembergia, cup flower

Oregano

Papaver, Iceland poppy

Parsley

Petunia

Phlox, annual phlox, moss pinks

Portulaca, rose moss

Salvia, scarlet sage

Sanvitalia, creeping zinnia

Senecio, dusty miller

Stachys, lamb's ears

Tagetes, French marigold

Thyme

Torenia, wishbone flower

Tropaeolum, nasturtium

Verbena

Veronica, shorter varieties

Viola, pansy, Johnny jump-up

Zinnia, dwarf varieties

Plants for the Middle Ground

Achillea

Amaranthus, Joseph's coat

Anemone, Japanese anemone

Antirrhinum, tall snapdragons

Aquilegia, columbine

Artemisia

Aster

Astilbe

Basil

Calendula

Callistephus, China aster

Campanula, bellflower

Celosia

Chrysanthemum, garden mum, shasta daisy

Coreopsis

Cosmos

Dahlia

Dicentra, bleeding heart

Digitalis, foxglove

Gaillardia, blanket flower

Gladiolus, shorter varieties

Gypsophila, baby's breath

Helianthus, Heliopsis, sunflower

Hemerocallis, daylily

Heuchera, coralbells

Hibiscus

Hosta

Iris

Lantana

Lavender

Lilium, lily

Monarda, beebalm

Nepeta, catmint

Nicotiana

Paeonia, peony

Papaver, Iceland and oriental poppies

Pelargonium, geranium

Phlox, garden phlox

Platycodon, balloon flower

Rudbeckia, black-eyed Susan, gloriosa daisy

Salvia, mealycup sage

Sedum

Tagetes, African marigold

Veronica

Zinnia

Background Plants

Alcea, hollyhock

Amaranthus, love-lies-bleeding

Artemisia, tallest varieties

Aster, tallest varieties

Canna

Cleome, spider flower

Cosmos

Dahlia, tallest varieties

Digitalis, foxglove

Gladiolus

Hedera, English ivy

Helianthus, giant sunflower

Heliopsis, tallest varieties

Hemerocallis, daylily

Hibiscus

Ipomoea, morning glory

Lantana

Lilium, lily

Thunbergia, black-eyed Susan vine

Plants for Groundcovers and Carpets

Artemisia, low-growing varieties
Astilbe
Dianthus, garden pinks
Ferns
Festuca, dwarf blue fescue
Hemerocallis, daylily, for tall cover
Hosta
Impatiens
Lobularia, sweet alyssum
Myosotis, forget-me-not

Nepeta, catmint
Pachysandra
Phlox, moss pinks
Portulaca, rose moss
Sanvitalia, creeping zinnia
Stachys, lamb's ears
Thyme
Vinca
Viola, violet

Plants for Pots

Practically any plant will grow in a container, if the container is big enough. The plants on this list are at home in the smaller spaces offered by conventional flower pots and planters.

Sun

Ageratum
Antirrhinum, snapdragon
Basil
Begonia
Brachycome, Swan River daisy
Browallia
Calendula
Callistephus, China aster
Celosia
Chives
Chrysanthemum
Coleus
Dianthus
Dracaena
Eustoma, lisianthus
Fuchsia
Iberis, candytuft
Lobelia
Lobularia, sweet alyssum
Marjoram
Nicotiana

Nierembergia, cup flower
Oregano
Papaver, Iceland poppy
Parsley
Pelargonium, geranium
Petunia
Phlox, annual type
Portulaca, rose moss
Rosemary, young plants
Salvia
Sanvitalia, creeping zinnia
Senecio, dusty miller
Tagetes, marigold
Thyme
Torenia, wishbone flower
Tropaeolum, nasturtium
Verbena
Vinca, periwinkle
Viola, pansy, Johnny jump-up
Zinnia

Partial Shade or Shade

Begonia

Browallia

Callistephus, China aster

Coleus

Dracaena

Fuchsia

Hedera, English ivy

Impatiens

Lobelia

Lobularia, sweet alyssum

Nicotiana

Torenia, wishbone flower

Verbena

Vinca, periwinkle

Viola, pansy, Johnny jump-up

Hanging Basket Plants

Begonia

Brachycome, Swan River daisy

Browallia

Fuchsia

Hedera, English ivy

Impatiens

Ipomoea, dwarf morning glory

Pelargonium, ivy geranium, cascading geranium

Petunia, cascading varieties

Portulaca, rose moss

Sanvitalia, creeping zinnia

Thunbergia black-eyed Susan vine

Torenia, wishbone flower

Tropaeolum, climbing/trailing nasturtium

Verbena, sprawling varieties

Vinca, periwinkle

Plants for Windowboxes

Ageratum

Antirrhinum, dwarf snapdragon

Begonia

Brachycome, Swan River daisy

Browallia

Celosia, plume type

Chrysanthemum, marguerite

Dianthus, annual types

Iberis, globe candytuft

Impatiens

Lobelia

Lobularia, sweet alyssum

Marjoram

Myosotis, forget-me-not

Nierembergia, cup flower

Parsley

Pelargonium, geranium

Petunia

Phlox, annual type

Portulaca, rose moss

Salvia

Sanvitalia, creeping zinnia

Senecio, dusty miller

Tagetes, French marigold

Thyme

Torenia, wishbone flower

Tropaeolum, nasturtium

Verbena

Vinca, periwinkle

Viola, pansy, Johnny jump-up

Zinnia, dwarf zinnia

Plants for Shady Places

The plants on this list prefer or tolerate varying degrees of shade. Consult Chapter Five for details.

Ageratum

Anemone, Japanese anemone

Aquilegia, columbine

Astilbe

Begonia

Browallia

Brunnera Siberian bugloss

Caladium, elephant's ear

Callistephus, China aster

Campanula, bellflower

Chives

Cleome, spider flower

Coleus

Dicentra, bleeding heart

Digitalis, foxglove

Dracaena

Fuchsia

Hedera, English ivy

Hemerocallis, daylily

Heuchera, coralbells

Hosta

Impatiens

Lilium, lily

Lobelia

Lobularia, sweet alyssum

Monarda, beebalm

Myosotis, forget-me-not

Nepeta, catmint

Nicotiana

Nierembergia, cup flower

Pachysandra

Paeonia, peony

Papaver, poppy

Parsley

Platycodon, balloon flower

Rudbeckia, black-eyed Susan

Sedum 'Autumn Joy'

Stachys, lamb's ears

Torenia, wishbone flower

Verbena

Vinca, periwinkle

Viola, pansy, Johnny jump-up, violet

Drought-Tolerant Plants

These plants can tolerate varying degrees of dryness.

Achillea

Artemisia

Cleome, spider flower

Cosmos

Dianthus, some varieties

Helianthus, sunflower

Heliopsis, sunflower

Hemerocallis, daylily

Iberis, annual candytuft

Lantana

Lavender

Marjoram

Nepeta, catmint

Oregano

Pelargonium, zonal geranium

Portulaca, rose moss

Rosemary

Rudbeckia, black-eyed Susan, gloriosa daisy

Sedum

Senecio, dusty miller

Thyme

Yucca

Foliage Plants

Amaranthus, Joseph's coat

Artemisia

Basil

Caladium, elephant's ear

Chives

Coleus

Dracaena

Festuca, dwarf blue fescue

Hedera, English ivy

Hosta

Marjoram

Oregano

Pachysandra

Parsley

Rosemary

Senecio, dusty miller

Stachys, lamb's ears

Thyme

Vinca, periwinkle

Yucca

Flowers for Cutting

Achillea

Alcea, hollyhock

Amaranthus, love-lies-bleeding

Anemone, Japanese anemone

Antirrhinum, snapdragon

Aquilegia, columbine

Aster

Astilbe

Calendula

Callistephus, China aster

Campanula, bellflower

Celosia

Chrysanthemum

Cleome, spider flower

Coreopsis

Cosmos

Dahlia

Dianthus

Digitalis, foxglove

Eustoma, lisianthus

Gaillardia, blanket flower

Gladiolus

Gypsophila, baby's breath

Helianthus, sunflower

Heliopsis, sunflower

Heuchera, coralbells

Iberis, globe candytuft

Iris

Lantana

Lilium, lily

Monarda, beebalm

Nicotiana

Paeonia, peony

Papaver, poppy

Petunia

Phlox, garden phlox

Platycodon, balloon flower

Rudbeckia, black-eyed Susan, gloriosa daisy

Salvia

Tagetes, marigold

Tropaeolum, nasturtium

Verbena

Veronica

Zinnia

Fragrant Flowers and Plants

Basil, leaves

Dianthus, garden pinks

Lavender, flowers and leaves

Lilium, lily

Lobularia, sweet alyssum

Marjoram, leaves

Monarda, beebalm

Nepeta, catmint, leaves

Nicotiana alata, species form

Oregano, leaves

Paeonia, peony

Petunia

Phlox, garden phlox

Rosemary, leaves

Thyme, leaves

Tropaeolum, nasturtium

Red, Rose, and Pink Flowers

Achillea

Ageratum

Alcea, hollyhock

Amaranthus, love-lies-bleeding

Anemone, Japanese anemone

Antirrhinum, snapdragon

Aquilegia, columbine

Aster

Astilbe

Begonia

Callistephus, China aster

Campanula, bellflower

Canna

Celosia

Chives

Chrysanthemum, garden mum

Cleome, spider flower

Cosmos

Dahlia

Dianthus, garden pinks

Dicentra, bleeding heart

Digitalis, foxglove

Eustoma, lisianthus

Fuchsia

Gladiolus

Gypsophila, baby's breath

Hemerocallis, daylily

Heuchera, coralbells

Hibiscus

Iberis, annual candytuft

Impatiens

Ipomoea, morning glory

Iris

Lantana

Lilium, lily

Lobelia

Lobularia, sweet alyssum

Monarda, beebalm

Nicotiana

Paeonia, peony

Papaver, poppy

Pelargonium, geranium

Petunia

Phlox

Platycodon, balloon flower

Portulaca, rose moss

Salvia, scarlet sage

Sedum

Torenia, wishbone flower

Tropaeolum, nasturtium

Verbena

Veronica

Viola, pansy

Zinnia

Orange, Peach, and Salmon Flowers

Antirrhinum, snapdragon

Calendula

Canna

Celosia

Chrysanthemum

Cosmos

Dahlia

Dianthus, garden pinks

Gladiolus

Helianthus

Hemerocallis, daylily

Impatiens

Iris

Lantana

Lilium, lily

Papaver, poppy

Pelargonium, geranium

Phlox, annual phlox

Portulaca, rose moss

Sedum

Tagetes, marigold

Thunbergia, black-eyed Susan vine

Viola, pansy

Zinnia

Yellow and Gold Flowers

Achillea

Alcea, hollyhock

Antirrhinum, snapdragon

Aquilegia, columbine

Begonia, Reiger begonia

Calendula

Canna

Celosia

Chrysanthemum, garden mum, marguerite

Coreopsis

Cosmos

Dahlia

Gaillardia, blanketflower

Gladiolus

Helianthus, sunflower

Heliopsis, sunflower

Hemerocallis, daylily

Hibiscus

Iris

Lantana

Lilium, lily

Papaver, Iceland poppy

Petunia

Portulaca, rose moss

Rudbeckia, black-eyed Susan, gloriosa daisy

Sanvitalia, creeping zinnia

Tagetes, marigold

Thunbergia, black-eyed Susan vine

Tropaeolum, nasturtium

Verbena

Viola, pansy

Zinnia

Blue, Violet, Purple, and Lavender Flowers

Ageratum

Antirrhinum, snapdragon

Aquilegia, columbine

Aster

Brachycome, Swan River daisy

Browallia

Brunnera, Siberian bugloss

Callistephus, China aster

Campanula, bellflower

Chrysanthemum, garden mum

Cleome, spider flower

Dahlia

Digitalis, foxglove

Eustoma, lisianthus

Fuchsia

Gladiolus

Hosta

Iberis, globe candytuft

Impatiens

Ipomoea, morning glory

Iris

Lavender

Lobelia

Lobularia, sweet alyssum

Myosotis, forget-me-not

Nepeta, catmint

Nicotiana

Nierembergia, cup flower

Pelargonium, geranium

Petunia

Phlox

Platycodon, balloon flower

Rosemary

Salvia

Torenia, wishbone flower

Verbena

Veronica

Vinca, periwinkle

Viola, pansy, Johnny jump-up

White Flowers

Achillea

Ageratum

Alcea, hollyhock

Anemone, Japanese anemone

Antirrhinum, snapdragon

Aquilegia, columbine

Aster

Astilbe

Begonia

Browallia

Callistephus, China aster

Campanula, bellflower

Chrysanthemum, garden mum, marguerite, shasta daisy

Cleome, spider flower

Cosmos

Dahlia

Dianthus, garden pink

Dicentra, bleeding heart

Digitalis, foxglove

Eustoma, lisianthus

Gladiolus

Gypsophila, baby's breath

Heuchera, coralbells

Hibiscus

Hosta

Iberis, perennial candytuft

Iris

Lilium, lily

Lobelia

Lobularia, sweet alyssum

Monarda, beebalm

Myosotis, forget-me-not

Nepeta, catmint

Nicotiana

Nierembergia, cup flower

Paeonia, peony

Papaver, poppy

Pelargonium, geranium

Petunia

Phlox

Platycodon, balloon flower

Portulaca, rose moss

Salvia, mealycup sage

Tagetes, marigold

Thunbergia, black-eyed Susan vine

Torenia, wishbone flower

Tropaeolum, nasturtium

Verbena

Veronica

Vinca, periwinkle

Viola, pansy

Zinnia

Glossary

Analogous colors: Related, harmonious colors.

Annual: A plant that completes its entire life cycle, from seed to mature plant and production of new seeds, in a single growing season.

Axis: An imaginary straight line around which all or part of a garden design is arranged.

Biennial: A plant that lives for two years, beginning growth in the first year, blooming, setting seeds, and dying the second year. Many biennials will bloom the first year from seed and can be grown as annuals.

Border: A garden area that is longer than it is wide, and may be used to divide or separate parts of the landscape.

Calyx: The outer "envelope" of a flower, consisting of individual sepals, which encloses the bud before it opens.

Complementary colors: Colors located opposite one another on an artist's color wheel; the strongest possible color contrast.

Compost: A mixture of decomposed organic wastes that have been piled and turned periodically to hasten decomposition, used to condition garden soil and add nutrients and organic matter.

Corm: A solid, bulblike structure that is actually the enlarged base of a stem. Gladiolus and crocus are two plants that grow from corms rather than true bulbs.

Crown: The point on a plant where the roots meet the main stem.

Cultivar: Shortened form of cultivated variety, indicating a variety developed in cultivation, which may or may not be reproducible from seed.

Deadhead: Remove faded and dead flowers from a plant; an important grooming technique. Regular deadheading encourages prolonged blooming in many plants.

Divided: Term used to describe leaves or leaflets with lobed or cut edges that give them a delicate, lacy appearance; appearing to be divided into separate segments.

Division: A method of propagation involving cutting apart or separating root clumps of perennials to make several new plants from one mature plant.

Drift: A curved, soft-edged clump of plants; the most attractive, naturalistic planting pattern for large flower beds and borders.

Genus: A group of closely related plant species, with common characteristics.

Groundcover: A spreading or trailing plant intended to cover or carpet an expanse of soil. Although most groundcover plants are low-growing, such as vinca and lawn grasses, taller plants of spreading habit, such as daylilies and ornamental grasses, can also be used for this purpose.

Half-hardy: Able to withstand occasional light frost, but damaged or killed by prolonged exposure to subfreezing temperatures.

Hardening-off: A process by which transplants started indoors are gradually acclimatized to outdoor conditions before they are transplanted into the garden.

Hardy: Able to withstand the coldest winter temperatures and the hottest summer temperatures in a given location without protection.

Humus: Decayed plant and animal matter that is very beneficial to garden soil; also called organic matter.

Island bed: A freestanding garden bed that can be viewed from all sides.

Leaf axil: The point where the leaf stem (petiole) meets a plant stem or branch.

Loam: Soil that contains a mixture of sand, silt, and clay particles, and usually enough organic matter and minerals to be naturally fertile; the ideal garden soil.

Microclimate: The local environment in and around the garden.

Mulch: An organic or inorganic material used to cover the soil surface between and around plants in a garden.

Organic matter: Decomposed plant and animal matter; also known as humus.

Parterre: A flat area decorated with flower beds, often in elaborate shapes and usually outlined with a low hedge, intended to be viewed from overhead.

Perennial: A plant that lives longer than two years.

Perlite: A lightweight, white volcanic rock that has been expanded by heat; it can be added to potting media to lighten and aerate them.

Petiole: Leaf stem.

pH: The measure of a soil's acidity or alkalinity, expressed in numerical units of 0 to 14, with 7.0 being neutral.

Pinching: Removing the growing tip of branching plants to encourage bushier growth.

Polychromatic garden: A garden of flowers in mixed colors; a multicolored garden.

Resistant variety: A plant variety with natural or inbred ability to suffer less damage from a particular pest or disease than other plants of its kind.

Rhizome: An underground stem, usually growing horizontally.

Self-sow: Deposit seeds (when flowers are left to mature on the plant) that will produce new plants next year where they fall, with no help needed from the gardener.

Species: A group of closely related plants that are similar in structure, share a common heritage, and remain the same from one generation to the next.

Spike: A flower structure in which individual flowers are clustered along a vertical stem.

Strawberry jar: A tall pot with small side pockets for planting as well as the usual top opening.

Tender: Unable to tolerate any frost or freezing temperatures; tender plants need warm conditions in order to grow well.

Variegated: Leaves that are striped, blotched, streaked, mottled, or otherwise marked with a color different from their ground color, which in most plants is green.

Variety: A naturally occurring variant of a species, different from the species in size, flower or leaf color, growth habit, or other characteristics. The term is often used informally to refer to cultivars as well as true botanical varieties.

Vermiculite: Lightweight particles of mica expanded by heat; added to potting mixtures to lighten the texture and improve moisture retention.

Windbreak: A barrier between the garden and prevailing winds, which protects plants by decreasing the force of the wind hitting them.

Recommended Reading

Clausen, Ruth Rogers and Nicolas H. Ekstrom, *Perennials for American Gardens.* New York: Random House, 1989

Halpin, Anne Moyer, *Foolproof Planting.* Emmaus, PA: Rodale Press, Inc., 1990

Halpin, Anne M., *The Window Box Book.* New York: Simon & Schuster, 1989

Harper, Pamela J., *Designing with Perennials.* New York: Macmillan Publishing Company, 1991

Heriteau, Jacqueline, *The American Horticultural Society Flower Finder.* New York: Simon & Schuster, 1992

Johnson, Hugh, *The Principles of Gardening.* New York: Fireside Books, 1979

Loewer, Peter, *The Annual Garden.* Emmaus, PA: Rodale Press, Inc., 1988

Loewer, Peter, *Tough Plants for Tough Places.* Emmaus, PA: Rodale Press, Inc., 1992

McGourty, Frederick, *The Perennial Gardener.* Boston: Houghton Mifflin Co., 1989

Plants and Gardens handbook series. Brooklyn, NY: Brooklyn Botanic Garden. Helpful handbooks on a host of gardening topics, written and edited by experts.

Rodale's Illustrated Encyclopedia of Herbs. Emmaus, PA: Rodale Press, Inc., 1987

Taylor's Guides to *Annuals, Herbs, Perennials.* Boston: Houghton Mifflin Co. A series of well-illustrated guides to particular types of plants.

Wyman, Donald, *Wyman's Gardening Encyclopedia.* New York: Macmillan Publishing Company, 1987

An Index of Common Plant Names

Adam's needle, *Yucca*
African marigold, *Tagetes*
Allwood pink, *Dianthus*
Althaea, *Alcea*
Alyssum, *Lobularia*
American marigold, *Tagetes*

Baby's breath, *Gypsophila*
Balloon flower, *Platycodon*
Basil, *Ocimum*
Bearded iris, *Iris*
Bedding geranium, *Pelargonium*
Beebalm, *Monarda*
Bellflower, *Campanula*
Bergamot, *Monarda*
Black-eyed Susan, *Rudbeckia*
Black-eyed Susan vine, *Thunbergia*
Blanket flower, *Gaillardia*
Bleeding heart, *Dicentra*
Bugloss, *Brunnera*

Candytuft, *Iberis*
Canterbury bells, *Campanula*
Catmint, *Nepeta*
Cheddar pink, *Dianthus*
Chives, *Allium*
Clock vine, *Thunbergia*
Columbine, *Aquilegia*
Coralbells, *Heuchera*
Coneflower, *Rudbeckia*
Cranesbill, *Geranium*
Creeping zinnia, *Sanvitalia*
Cup flower, *Nierembergia*

Daisy, *Brachycome, Chrysanthemum, Rudbeckia*
Daylily, *Hemerocallis*
Dusty miller, *Senecio*

Edging lobelia, *Lobelia*
Elephant's ear, *Caladium*
English ivy, *Hedera*
English lavender, *Lavandula*

False spirea, *Astilbe*
Fescue, *Festuca*
Fibrous-rooted begonia, *Begonia*
Flossflower, *Ageratum*
Flowering tobacco, *Nicotiana*
Forget-me-not, *Myosotis*
Foxglove, *Digitalis*
French marigold, *Tagetes*
Fringed bleeding heart, *Dicentra*

Garden mum, *Chrysanthemum*
Garden phlox, *Phlox*
Garden pink, *Dianthus*
Garden verbena, *Verbena*
Geranium, *Pelargonium*
Globe candytuft, *Iberis*
Gloriosa daisy, *Rudbeckia*
Grass pink, *Dianthus*
Greek oregano, *Origanum*

Harebell, *Campanula*
Hollyhock, *Alcea*

Iceland poppy, *Papaver*
Ivy, *Hedera*
Ivy geranium, *Pelargonium*

Japanese anemone, *Anemone*
Johnny jump-up, *Viola*
Joseph's coat, *Amaranthus*

Lamb's ears, *Stachys*
Lavender, *Lavandula*

Lily, *Lilium*
Lisianthus, *Eustoma*
Love-lies-bleeding, *Amaranthus*

Marguerite, *Chrysanthemum*
Marigold, *Tagetes*
Marjoram, *Origanum*
Mealycup sage, *Salvia*
Milfoil, *Achillea*
Morning glory, *Ipomoea*
Moss pink, *Phlox*
Mountain pink, *Phlox*
Mum, *Chrysanthemum*
Myrtle, *Vinca*

Nasturtium, *Tropaeolum*

Oregano, *Origanum*
Oriental poppy, *Papaver*
Oswego tea, *Monarda*

Pansy, *Viola*
Parsley, *Petroselinum*
Peony, *Paeonia*
Periwinkle, *Vinca*
Pinks, *Dianthus, Phlox*
Plantain lily, *Hosta*
Poppy, *Papaver*
Pot marigold, *Calendula*
Prairie gentian, *Eustoma*

Reiger begonia, *Begonia*
Rose mallow, *Hibiscus*
Rosemary, *Rosmarinus*
Rose moss, *Portulaca*

Sage, *Salvia*
Scarlet sage, *Salvia*
Shasta daisy, *Chrysanthemum*
Siberian bugloss, *Brunnera*
Siberian iris, *Iris*
Siver king, *Artemisia*
Silver mound, *Artemisia*
Snapdragon, *Antirrhinum*
Speedwell, *Veronica*
Spider flower, *Cleome*
Stonecrop, *Sedum*
Summer phlox, *Phlox*
Sunflower, *Helianthus, Heliopsis*
Swan River daisy, *Brachycome*
Sweet alyssum, *Lobularia*
Sweet marjoram, *Origanum*
Sweet violet, *Viola*
Sweet William, *Dianthus*

Tasselflower, *Amaranthus*
Thyme, *Thymus*

Violet, *Viola*

Wax begonia, *Begonia*
Wishbone flower, *Torenia*
Woolflower, *Celosia*

Yarrow, *Achillea*
Yellow sage, *Lantana*

Zonal geranium, *Pelargonium*

Index

Boldface page numbers indicate art.

Achillea (yarrow)
  designing with, 41, 59–61
  guide to, 94–95
  uses for, 133, 135, 138–142
Acidic soils, 24
Ageratum (flossflower)
  designing with, **19**, 42, 58, 59
  guide to, 95
  uses for, 133, 134, 136–138, 140, 142
Ajuga, 61
Alcea (hollyhock)
  designing with, 44, 52, 57
  guide to, 95
  uses for, 135, 139–142
Alkaline soils, 24
Amaranthus (love-lies-bleeding; Joseph's coat)
  guide to, 95–96
  uses for, 135, 139, 140
Analogous color schemes, 38–39
Anemone (Japanese anemone)
  guide to, 96
  uses for, 135, 138–140, 142
Annual phlox, 42
Annuals
  deadheading, 86
  designing with, 29, 38, 42
  hardiness of, 74
Antirrhinum (snapdragon)
  deadheading, 86
  designing with, 41, 42, 47, 53, 54, 59, 61
  guide to, 96
  uses for, 134–137, 139–142
Aphids, 65, 89, 90
Aquilegia (columbine)
  designing with, 41, 50, **56**
  guide to, 96–97
  uses for, 135, 138–142
Arbors, 59, **61**
Artemisia, 61
  guide to, 97
  uses for, 133–136, 138, 139

Aster
  deadheading, 86
  designing with, 41
  guide to, 97–98
  uses for, 133, 135, 139, 140, 142
Astilbe (false spirea)
  designing with, 41, 42, **56**
  guide to, 98
  uses for, 133, 135, 136, 138–140, 142
Azaleas, 24

Bacillus thuriniensis, 89
Background plants, 135
Bark chips, 84
Basil, 48
  guide to, 98–99
  pinching, 86
  uses for, 135, 136, 139, 140
Beds
  carpet, **51**
  circular, **33**, 34, 51, **52**, 53
  continuity of design, 31, 34
  defined, 31
  formal, **19**, 31, 44, 51–**52**
  island, **19**, 53
  naturalistic, 19–20
  oval, 53
  raised, 24, **33**
  rectangular, **32**, 34
  for small spaces, **46**, 47, 50–**51**
  half-moon, **56**
  south-facing, 25
  terraced, **33**, 34, 44
Begonia (wax begonia; Reiger begonia)
  designing with, 42, 48, 51–**53**, **54**
  guide to, 99
  uses for, 42, 134, 136–138, 140–142
Blood meal, 71, 72
Blooming times, 42
Blue flowers, 142
Bone meal, 77